Japan's Pa

an introd

HANS H. B/
Professor of Pol
University of California, Los Angeles

Japan's Parliament, or Diet, tends to be perceived from one of two widely divergent perspectives. On the one hand, it is made to appear as an institution operating according to parliamentary norms, as epitomized by the British model. On the other hand, it is denigrated as being nothing more than the setting for periodic scenes of violence. This introductory study is intended to provide a less stereotyped assessment of this national legislature.

Some ten years have gone into the process of researching the subject. Extensive periods of residence in Japan allowed the author to observe the Diet in action, to interview (in Japanese) many of its members, their administrative assistants, the Diet's Secretariat, Japanese newsmen whose task is to report the legislative process, and Japanese political scientists. Insofar as possible, a conscious effort was made to avoid American and European biases and to present the Diet as an institution operating within Japanese society.

A variety of forces have shaped the Diet, which is still in the process of institutional evolution. Japan's political party system, especially the influence of factionalism, is discussed as a major determinant of what can — and cannot — be accomplished in the Diet. Another set of constraints and opportunities is seen in the Diet's internal machinery, especially its rules of procedure. These feed into a discussion of the means by which the majority party and its varied forces of opposition seek to manipulate the written and unwritten rules of the game to their respective advantage. Each of these aspects is recapitulated in a conclusion assessing the Diet's viability as a parliamentary institution.

Japan's Parliament:
an introduction

Japan's Parliament:

an introduction

HANS H. BAERWALD

Professor of Political Science
University of California at Los Angeles

CAMBRIDGE UNIVERSITY PRESS

Published by the Syndics of the Cambridge University Press
Bentley House, 200 Euston Road, London NW1 2DB
American Branch: 32 East 57th Street, New York, N.Y. 10022

© Cambridge University Press 1974

Library of Congress Catalogue Card Number: 73-90810

ISBN 0 521 20387 2

First published 1974
Photoset in Malta by St Paul's Press Ltd
Printed in the United States of America

For DI-AN-JA-DA

Contents

Preface and acknowledgments

This brief study of Japan's parliament has been under preparation for ten years. Initially, I had hoped to write a book that would be in accord with my ethnic heritage — long, infinitely detailed, and so heavy a tome that only the most dedicated masochist would read it. Instead, this slim volume emphasizes what I believe are the Diet's most important features. It is my hope that this will lead to further studies because the literature on the Diet remains sparse.

Hence, my basic purpose has been to write an introduction and to answer certain questions: (1) What are the Diet's origins and how does this heritage affect its place in Japanese politics? (2) What are the features of Japan's political parties that affect the manner of their operations in the Diet? (3) How is the Diet organized internally and how do its rules of procedure affect its capacity to fulfill its constitutional mandate: to be Japan's supreme legislative organ? (4) Why is the Diet the scene of turmoil periodically? (5) What general conclusions, tentative though they might be, can be made about the Diet as a parliamentary institution?

The questions are seemingly easy, but the attempt to find answers has taken far longer than might have been expected. One of the reasons is that I have relied very heavily on personal interviews and observation. My decision to utilize this research technique was based in part on the paucity of literature on the Diet as well as my finding the process of being an observer to be enjoyable. It was, however, time-consuming. None of it would have been possible without the marvelous goodwill and cooperation of many individuals.

Many academic foundations and universities have assisted me. My initial efforts in 1963 were made possible by a grant from the joint committee of the American Council of Learned Societies and the Social Science Research Council. This was supplemented by a generous stipend from the Rockefeller Foundation (1965–7). Two terms as director of the University of California's Tokyo Study Center under the auspices of the University's Education Abroad Program allowed my family and me to spend a total of three years at the International

Christian University in Tokyo. Several travel grants from UCLA's Committee on Research and the Committee on International and Comparative Studies permitted some brief trips to Japan to study current political developments. To all of these institutions and their officials I express my gratitude for their financial support, without which nothing would have been possible.

I am also grateful to the administration, faculty and students at International Christian University (ICU). They welcomed my family, the University of California students and me with kindness and consideration even though their academy was in the midst of serious crises to which our presence — especially in 1969–70 — added its own turmoil. That experience taught me much; far more than I was able to contribute to ICU's academic program. I am particularly grateful for the understanding of my friends regarding my predicament in the autumn of 1969. Not only mercury poisoning is the cause of 'itai-itai byō', broadly defined.

All of these trips to and periods of residence in Japan assisted me in learning about, and observing the Diet over time. They also made me cautious. It is not without reason that the oft-repeated story is told: spend a few weeks in Japan and you can write a book; spend a year and you still might be able to write a respectable article; spend any more time than that and you would be best advised to write nothing because there is no excuse any more for being so abysmally ignorant. Of course, having been born in Japan, having spent the better part of my youth there and having been there for two and a half years during the Occupation made it all the more painful.

These periods of residence in Japan were helpful, but they would have meant little without the generous assistance of many Japanese individuals who did their best to teach me about their contemporary politics. It is impossible for me to mention all of them and for this I apologize and most sincerely ask for their understanding. I am also concerned that some of what they taught me might be held against them. Nonetheless, my debt to them is so great that it would be totally impolite not to acknowledge their immense contribution.

In the summer of 1963, it was my extremely good fortune to arrive with an introduction to Mr Sasakawa Takeo who was then covering the Foreign Ministry for the *Sankei Shimbun* (newspaper). He undertook the task of introducing me to his many news media colleagues, including the then director of his paper's political section, Mr Yoshimura Toru, and his successors Mr Kitahata Michio and Mr Yamane Takuo as well as all the other *Sankei* political reporters. Together they introduced me to the intricate network of communications inside the world of Japanese politics and the news media — a fascinating subject in its own right.

It was Mr Sasakawa who was willing to risk introducing this *gaijin* (foreigner) to the *yo-mawari* (night-rounds), a hallowed Japanese news gathering effort, that enabled me to meet Mr Ohira Masayoshi (Minister for Foreign Affairs in the Cabinets of Ikeda Hayato and Tanaka Kakuei) and Mr Fukuda Takeo (Minister of State in many Cabinets), both of whom have taught me so much over the intervening years. It was also Mr Sasakawa who introduced me to Mr Obata Shin'ichi (of the *Sankei Shimbun*) who in turn arranged for me to be an observer at a seminar of the faction led by the late Mr Kawashima Shōjirō, former Vice-President of the LDP.

Others in the *Sankei Shimbun*'s political section were extremely helpful in making it possible to receive permission to be an observer at Socialist Party Conventions, Democratic-Socialist Party Conventions and, much later, Komeitō Conventions. All of the *Sankei* reporters were willing to allow me to spend time with them in their various offices and clubs and let me sit with them while election returns were coming in or while important events were transpiring elsewhere — a television broadcast after midnight of the Nixon-Satō meeting in Washington announcing the reversion of Okinawa to Japan being among the most memorable. To all of them, my heartfelt thanks.

I am also deeply indebted to many staff members of the Diet Secretariat, especially Mr Okubo Kimio of the External Affairs Section in the House of Representatives. He and his colleagues were extremely gracious in making arrangements for me to be granted countless interviews with Members of the Diet and to observe committee meetings and plenary sessions. They were never irritated by many requests for favors even though I must have taken up an inordinate amount of their time. The same is true of the House of Representatives Secretariat's Committee Section, especially its then Deputy-chief Mr Ogyū Kei'ichi and his associates Mr Hirano Sadao and Mr Horiguchi Ichirō. They prepared special reports for me on the operations of the Diet's committee system that were invaluable.

Many Members of the Diet and their assistants have extended courtesies over the years. Minister of International Trade and Industry, Nakasone Yasuhirō, and his staff, Mr Utsunomiya Tokuma and his staff assistants, Mr Kawakami Tamio, Mr Iwano Miyoji of Deputy Prime Minister Miki Takeo's office, all of the staff members of Mr Ōhira's office and of the Kōchi-kai, the official name of the Ōhira faction, were particularly generous with their time and assistance.

Mr Watanabe Tsuneo of the *Yomiuri Shimbun* (newspaper) influenced me profoundly by his insight into the intricacies of factional politics, about which he is the acknowledged expert. To him and our mutual friends in the *kenkyu-kai* (study group), my heartfelt thanks for many a stimulating evening.

Japanese colleagues in the field of Political Science have also been most helpful. Professor Ishida Takeshi of Tokyo University encouraged me when others were doubtful about my project. Professor Watanabe Yasuo, Chairman of ICU's Graduate School of Public Administration, always had time for discussion and his sage counsel kept me from making too many errors. Professor Hashimoto Akira of Meiji University painstakingly reviewed my earlier essay on the Diet's committee system and his assistance on matters of interpretation and factual accuracy were invaluable. Professor Tomita Nobuo of Meiji University graciously helped me with all kinds of valuable material on elections as did Mr Nishihira Shigeki, whose statistical compilation of Japanese election is a gold mine of information. Professor Uchida Mitsuru of Waseda University joined me for several crucial interviews and was always friendly and helpful. Professor Uchiyama Shōzo of Hosei University always had a fresh perspective. Mr Sodei Rinjirō, a former student, was always willing to share views and search for material.

I also owe a profound debt of gratitude to two good friends who are American foreign correspondents in Japan. Mr Sam Jameson of the *Los Angeles Times* is a generous host, a true student of Japanese politics, and a kind critic. Mr Richard Halloran of the *New York Times* is an old friend, profoundly knowledgeable, and a superb editor. I owe both of them more than I can ever repay.

Throughout it all my family has been unbelievably patient. Diane and the children traveled with me to Japan and put up with the irregular schedule that is demanded of anyone who wants to learn about Japanese politics. Diane contributed immensely to the final product by translating what I had written into readable English. It is to her and the children that this book is dedicated.

Two final words. Japanese names are rendered in the vernacular style — family name first. Only I am to be held responsible for any errors of fact or interpretation.

Los Angeles
May 1973   HHB

CHAPTER ONE

From Imperial Diet to National Diet

'The *Teikoku Gikai* (Imperial Diet) shall consist of two Houses, a House of Peers and a House of Representatives.'[1] 'The Diet shall be the highest organ of state power, and shall be the sole law-making organ of the State.'[2] These two sentences express the fundamental distinction between the intentions of those who drafted Japan's two Constitutions — that of the Meiji Emperor in 1890 and that of the Supreme Commander of the Allied Powers Douglas MacArthur in 1947. If the first stressed structure, the second emphasizes power and authority. As an institution of government, the Imperial Diet survived a little over fifty-five years of a troubled and uncertain existence and the National Diet is in the second quarter century of its efforts to fulfill its Constitutional mandate.

Formal Constitutional and informal political constraints impeded the Imperial Diet from becoming a representative assembly and parliamentary body exercising legislative power. The Meiji Constitution provided that 'the *Tenno⁻* [Emperor] exercises the legislative power with the consent of the *Teikoku Gikai*.'[3] Additionally, Cabinet Ministers were formally responsible to the Emperor rather than to parliament.[4] Like its present parliamentary namesake, it was bicameral. The House of Peers buttressed the formal authority of the imperial institution with a membership consisting of the imperial family, the hereditary nobility and others appointed by the Emperor. Only the House of Representatives was popularly elected, initially by a severely limited portion of the public — those who paid fifteen yen or more in taxes, at the time a significant sum — and after 1925 on the basis of universal suffrage of all male citizens twenty-five years and older. Women were excluded from the franchise.

[1] The 'Meiji' Constitution, Chapter III, Article XXXIII, Fujii Shin'ichi, *The Constitution of Japan, A Historical Survey* (Tokyo: The Hokuseido Press, 1965), p. 302.
[2] The 1947 Constitution, Chapter IV, Article 41, *ibid.*, p. 314.
[3] The 'Meiji' Constitution, Chapter I, Article V, *ibid.*, p. 299.
[4] The 'Meiji' Constitution, Chapter IV, Article LV, *ibid.*, p. 305.

1

From the point of view of constitutional doctrine, the Emperor was all-powerful. It was he who exercised legislative power, who sanctioned laws and had them administered, who convoked the Diet and dissolved the House of Representatives, who was at the apex of the civil and military bureaucratic organization of the government, who declared war, made peace, and concluded treaties.[1] These provisions of the Meiji Consitution established a powerful wall against those who sought to make the Imperial Diet into something more than a facade.

It is of course a fiction of the Meiji Constitution that the Emperor actually ruled. Several groups exercised power — Army and Navy officers; the senior echelons of the civilian bureaucracy; financiers and industrialists; the Privy Councillors (the Emperor's formal advisors); the *Genrō*, or elder statesmen, who had been Prime Ministers of earlier Cabinets. All had shares of political power and some, notably the military, even acted independently. Simultaneously, all could — and when the occasion demanded or when they found it useful to do so did — claim that they were acting in accordance with the will of the Emperor. It proved to be an insurmountable barrier for anyone who claimed to be articulating the views of ordinary voters.

Agitation on behalf of popular rights and representative assemblies antedated the Meiji Constitution and its Imperial Diet, which were at least in part a response to ideas espoused by participants in the Jiyu-Minken Undō (movement on behalf of liberty and people's rights) in the 1880s. Organizations which later became political parties also came into existence as early as the 1870s. They gradually became more effective, but most of them appealed to and were reflections of a narrow spectrum of public attitudes and aspirations, especially prior to the enactment of the Universal Manhood Suffrage Law of 1925. Even after that, minor left-wing parties such as the Nihon Shakai Taishu-Tō (Japan Social Mass Party) never acquired more than minimal representation (less than 10 percent) in the lower House of the Diet. Their leaders, who tried to organize the rural tenant farmers and urban factory workers, were harassed by police forces, spent endless time and prodigious energy in ideological debates, and were generally ineffectual. By contrast, the major political parties of the decades between the First and Second World Wars — the Seiyukai and the Minseitō —

---

[1] The 'Meiji' Constitution, Chapter I, Articles V–VII, X–XIII, *ibid.*, pp. 299–300.

reflected the interests and were subordinate to the dictates of the *zaibatsu* (financial–industrial clique).[1]

Furthermore, there was no tradition of popular participation in government or politics. *'Kanson Minpi'* (officials are to be revered, the people despised) was a slogan summarizing age-old traditions which were intensified by strong feelings for hierarchy and class. A follower (*kobun*) was to be loyal to his master (*oyabun*); a junior (*kohai*), either in age or experience, was subordinate to his senior (*senpai*); and a student (*deshi*) never questioned the wisdom of his teacher (*sensei*). These relationships were mutually beneficial. An *oyabun* would take care of his *kobun* in a paternalistic fashion. Often, a subordinate official would do the hard work for his senior, who would merely ratify the recommendations by adding his seal (*hankō*). It was not at all unusual for a junior official to draft a detailed policy proposal or law amendment and to see that it would receive approval as it made its way up the hierarchy, so that by the time the document reached the desk of the senior official it was festooned with red seals of concurrence. This system — called *ringisei*[2] frequently made a puppet of the senior official. It also allowed everyone to disclaim personal responsibility; after all, everyone had participated, everyone had agreed, so why challenge the painstakingly determined consensus or feel a personal sense of embarrassment if the proposal proved to be disastrous in its consequences?

This listing of constitutional, political, and sociocultural constraints could be expanded almost *ad infinitum* in assessing why the Imperial Diet remained an ineffective and ineffectual center of power. Nonetheless, there were some contrary developments. For example, Japanese historians have stressed the rise of democratic tendencies during the reign of the Taishō Emperor (1912–26). The Japanese were industrializing rapidly; the First World War afforded them a tremendous opportunity to expand their overseas commercial markets; there was intellectual ferment in the universities; political parties, aided and abetted by the new-found wealth of the business community, expanded their activities; a commoner-politician, Hara Kei, became Prime Minister,

[1]Robert A. Scalapino, *Democracy and the Party Movement in Prewar Japan* (Berkeley and Los Angeles: University of California Press, 1953). George O. Totten III, *The Social Democratic Movement in Prewar Japan* (New Haven: Yale University Press, 1966).

[2]Tsuji Kiyoaki, 'Decision-Making in the Japanese Government: A Study of "Ringisei"', in Robert E. Ward, ed., *Political Development in Modern Japan* (Princeton, N.J.: Princeton University Press, 1968), pp. 457–75.

and the increasing level of public participation in politics was accorded recognition in the passage of the 1925 law enfranchising all adult males.[1]

The mental incompetence of the reigning Emperor was one of those historical accidents that probably, as in the case of England's King George III, had marginal consequences; if the Emperor was unfit to rule, it would not be difficult to begin asking questions privately and discreetly, about the aura of mystical superiority that surrounded the imperial institution and its manipulators. At the time, raising such doubts was to indulge in 'dangerous thoughts' which — if done publicly — could lead to a visit from the Special Higher (Thought Control) Police and terms in jail for having violated the provisions of the *Chian Iji-Hō* (Peace Preservation Law). The Japanese people enjoyed more freedom in the Taishō era than before or after it prior to the postwar period, but it was still a circumscribed freedom.

This limited experiment with democracy proved to be abortive. Despite its limitations and its short duration, however, some politicians became used to electoral politics and to working in the House of Representatives. Many of them acquired a sense of pride in their institutional home and their profession. Many of them might have been corrupt, as was repeatedly alleged, in that they were excessively dependent on financial contributions from big business. But this was less significant than the experience they gained as parliamentarians; they provided a pool of talent for membership in the postwar National Diet.

The militarists, who were ascendant in Japanese politics in the 1930s, were sufficiently worried about the active politicians in the Diet to want to bring them, and the institution itself, to heel. Military officers were able to promote their cherished goal of achieving greater national unity by forcing the political parties to commit suicide. In their stead, the Imperial Rule Assistance Association: IRAA (Taisei Yokusan-kai) and its various subsidiaries such as the Imperial Rule Assistance Political Society were established. Whether the IRAA is to be perceived as an instrument for the creation of a quasi-fascist state in Japan or as an organization through which politicians, by uniting in it, could retain some power *vis-à-vis* the military remains a question for further historical inquiry.

[1]For brief and thought-provoking analyses of factors influencing Japanese politics and behavior, please see Ishida Takeshi, *Japanese Society* (New York: Random House, 1971), and Nakane Chie, *Japanese Society* (Berkeley and Los Angeles: University of California Press, 1970). It is to be regretted that both books have the same title, as their contents are different.

The Imperial Diet was not abolished. An election for the House of Representatives was conducted in 1942, at the height of Japanese successes in what they designate the 'War in the Pacific Ocean' (*Taiheiyō Sensō*). It was not an open or free election inasmuch as preference was given to IRAA-endorsed candidates, who could be expected to support Prime Minister Tojo and his military coalition. Three hundred seventy-five out of four hundred sixty-six of them were elected, leaving only a minority that might be, but apparently rarely were, critical of the government. These pantomimes of public participation in the political process made it possible for the facade, if not the substance, of electoral and parliamentary politics to survive even at the height of the militarist era. There is therefore a continuity between the Imperial Diet which had its birth in 1890 and the National Diet which came into existence in 1947.

The Occupation era

Japan's dream of a Pacific empire ended in the lethal ashes of Hiroshima and Nagasaki and the rubble of its industrial wealth. With their defeat in war the Japanese people, for the first time in their history, experienced a foreign occupation. The foreigners, most of whom came from the United States, brought with them plans to re-organize Japanese society and its political system. In paragraph ten of the Potsdam Declaration, which outlines the basic terms of surrender for Japan, the following goals were stated: 'The Japanese Government shall remove all obstacles to the revival and strengthening of democratic tendencies among the Japanese people. Freedom of speech, of religion, and of thought, as well as respect for the fundamental human rights shall be established.'[1]

Two American policy documents[2] provided detailed elaborations

---

[1]*Political Reorientation of Japan September 1945 to September 1948; Report of the Government Section, Supreme Commander for the Allied Powers* (Washington, D.C.: Government Printing Office, 1949), Vol. II, p. 413. Hereafter, this source — the most complete public collection of policy documents (in Volume II) and commentary (in Volume I) of the Occupation of Japan — will be referred to as *PRJ*.

[2]The first was prepared by a State-War-Navy Coordinating Committee (SWNCC) and was entitled 'United States Initial Post-Surrender Policy for Japan'. It was officially issued over President Truman's signature 6 September 1945. (For full text, please see *PRJ*, Vol. II, pp. 423—6.) The second was called 'Basic Initial Post-Surrender Directive to Supreme Commander for the Allied Powers for the Occupation and Control of Japan' and was issued by the American Joint Chiefs of Staff on 3 November 1945. (For full text, please see *PRJ*, Vol. II, pp. 428—39.)

of the Potsdam Declaration and became the guidelines for the reforms to be undertaken initially by the Supreme Command for the Allied Powers (SCAP), the organization that indirectly governed Japan for nearly seven years (September 1945 — April 1952). One crucial paragraph — the wording was similar in its essentials, but slightly different in minor details — which is to be found in both of these fundamental policy statements requires full quotation. It contains the essence of the policy that resulted in the establishment of the National Diet.

The ultimate objective of the United Nations with respect to Japan is to foster conditions which will give the greatest possible assurance that Japan will not again become a menace to the peace and security of the world and will permit her eventual admission as a responsible and peaceful member of the family of nations. Certain measures considered to be essential for the achievement of this objective have been set forth in the Potsdam Declaration. These measures include, among others ... the abolition of militarism and ultra-nationalism in all their forms; the disarmament and demilitarization of Japan, with continuing control over Japan's capacity to make war; the strengthening of democratic tendencies and processes in governmental, economic, and social institutions; and the encouragement of liberal political tendencies in Japan. The United States desires that the Japanese Government conform as closely as may be to principles of democratic self-government, but it is not the responsibility of the occupation forces to impose on Japan any form of government not supported by the freely expressed will of the people.[1]

These policy guidelines had a duality of objectives which were deeply intertwined during the first half of the Occupation. As far as possible, SCAP was to ensure that Japan would not again endanger the peace of the world. This was to be accomplished by demilitarization. Simultaneously, the Japanese people were to be encouraged to establish a democratic system of self-government. Implicit in these objectives was the belief that a pacifist Japan would be democratic, and that a democratic, self-governing Japan would not be militaristic. No other interpretation of these policy statements is plausible.[2]

It is easy to denigrate these objectives. They reflect a quaint innocence combined with considerable arrogance. They also reflect a refreshing optimism and self-confidence that the occupiers — all of whom were foreigners and many of whom had never been to Japan before — would be able to undertake for the people of Japan something that had eluded

[1] Joint Chiefs of Staff Directive, 'Basic, Initial Post Surrender Directive.' Part I, Paragraph 3a, *PRJ*, Vol. II, p. 429.
[2] Please see my *The Purge of Japanese Leaders under the Occupation* (Berkeley and Los Angeles: University of California Press, 1959); and Robert E. Ward, 'Reflections on the Allied Occupation and Planned Political Change in Japan', in Ward *Political Development in Modern Japan*, pp. 477–535.

them in over fifty years of experimentation with parliamentary democracy.

In retrospect, some confusion was inevitable in linking the twin objectives of demilitarization and democratization, which were simply assumed as being symbiotic in the basic documents which provided policy guidance to Supreme Commander MacArthur and his many subordinates. What gives me pause today is that as a participant in the enterprise at the time, it never occurred to me to question the now all too readily conceivable contradiction between these objectives. Quite the contrary was the case; I accepted the relationship between democracy and pacifism as being obvious. Such is the self-assurance and confidence of youth.

A doubtful and confusing, albeit high-minded, combination of premises and goals were included in the basic policies on which the vast superstructure of SCAP was built. That was probably its basic flaw, but there were others as well. First, few of the people brought in by them were conversant with Japan. This dearth of talent was exacerbated by General MacArthur's decision not to utilize many of the civil administrators who had been carefully trained in Japanese history, politics, and economic conditions. Many of them were sent to Korea instead. Rumor had it that General MacArthur was uncertain about their loyalty to him and his policies, but the Supreme Commander never had occasion to explain the motives for his decision. What was of consequence was that the talents of these excluded specialists were not fully utilized in Japan.

Second, a policy split developed between two major points of view inside SCAP's General Headquarters. One side took the Potsdam Declaration and the basic policy directives seriously. They believed that the principal mission of the Occupation was to assist the Japanese in democratizing their society and politics. Their opponents anticipated the then on-setting 'cold war' and were far more deeply interested in making Japan a stable bulwark against the rising threat of Communism in East Asia. For them, the zeal of the reformers was dangerous because it might lead to an even greater instability than that already present in the war-ravaged country. This conflict pitted two of the Occupation's most powerful personalities against each other. General Courtney Whitney, Chief of Government Section, [1] led the reformers;

[1] One of the Special Staff Sections in GHQ, SCAP; Government Section's mission was to advise the Supreme Commander on a broad range of issues relating to political reform. (For details, please see 'History of Government Section' in *PRJ*, Vol. II, pp. 790–821.) I was a language officer in this section, October 1946–February 1949.

whereas General Charles Willoughby, Assistant Chief of Staff G-2 (Intelligence) commanded the voices of caution, 'Nothing must be done to deteriorate ... the Occupation's astonishing tranquility; any move no matter how laudatory under the Potsdam Declaration must be analyzed as to its effects on public peace.'[1] This attitude undermined — sometimes subtly, sometimes blatantly — the goals of the SWNCC and JCS directives. As a Government Section loyalist my judgment is not entirely unbiased.

Within three years from the beginning of the Occupation (by the summer of 1948) this policy conflict in SCAP led to what the Japanese have termed the 'reverse course', that is to say, the Occupation's turning from the goals of demilitarization and reform to the objective of rebuilding Japan with only ancillary attention being given to 'the strengthening of democratic tendencies and processes'. The exact timing and specific content of this shift in overall policy orientation differed from one program to another. It is, however, undeniable that deviations from the post-surrender policies that were supposed to have guided the whole Occupation effort became more and more frequent with each passing year. It was palpably obvious to anyone who participated that the onsetting 'cold war', the disintegration of the Chinese Nationalist Government on the mainland and its removal to Taiwan in 1949, the Korean War which began in June of 1950, all contributed to diluting the self-confident and optimistic zeal that had characterized the initial policies.

It is interesting to note that these divisions over policy inside SCAP. came to be reflected in and absorbed by Japanese domestic politics. Occupation-sponsored reforms — whatever their internal contradictions, the shortness of time during which the Occupation accorded them primacy, and what the constraints imposed by administrative ineptitude may have done to limit their effectiveness — touched some deep aspirations (for and against) of the Japanese people. These changes assisted in altering the shape and substance of Japanese politics. For better or worse, the Diet emerged from it all as a different institution from what it had been in its earlier incarnation.

It is the new Constitution of Japan — it formally came into force on 3 May 1947 — which sets forth the fundamental institutional and other changes which distinguish the National Diet from the Imperial Diet.

---

[1]Memorandum to Government Section from the Assistant Chief of Staff G-2, 23 December 1946. Baerwald, *The Purge of Japanese Leaders under the Occupation*, p. 25.

After some false starts by various Japanese drafting committees, General MacArthur – on his own authority – established a working group inside the Government Section to prepare an initial draft of the document. The Supreme Commander acted independently of superior authorities in ordering his subordinates to do so, but the drafters scrupulously adhered to the SWNCC and JCS policy guidelines in its preparation. Numberless sessions between Japanese Government and Government Section representatives followed in order to refine its provisions and to translate it into the Japanese language, a task which can only be fully appreciated by anyone who has actually made an effort to come to understand both languages. An official Japanese Cabinet-sponsored draft was submitted to the Imperial Diet in June 1946, with the House of Representatives voting its final approval on 7 October 1946; in the interim it had also been discussed by the House of Peers and the Privy Council. An Imperial Rescript announced the new Constitution's formal promulgation as 'amendments of the Imperial Japanese Constitution'.[1]

Disagreements have surrounded the 1947 Constitution. Its actual paternity was deliberately hidden, in part because by making it appear to have been a Japanese-sponsored draft the whole issue of whether General MacArthur actually had the authority to order the preparation of a new constitution could thereby be obscured. After all, the initial post-surrender policy guidelines had provided for the encouragement of the freely-expressed will of the Japanese people, so long as it was in accordance with the principles of democratic self-government. Secondly, it allowed SCAP to avoid unnecessary entanglements with international supervisory councils which probably would have delayed the rapid preparation of the document. The Supreme Commander did not enjoy outsiders meddling in affairs which he believed to be in his domain. Third, propagating the fiction that the Constitution was Japanese in its origins would presumably enhance its acceptance by the Japanese public. It has been accepted and has survived the vicissitudes of over a quarter century, but not because anyone believes its origins to have been unsullied by foreign interference. The Constitution remains unamended because a sufficient set of domestic political

---

[1]*PRJ*, Vol. II, p. 670. Anyone interested in the official version of how the 1947 Constitution was drafted and approved will find the narrative history (*PRJ*, Vol. I, pp. 82–118) and the documentary collection (*PRJ*, Vol. II, pp. 586–683) to be informative, both for what is emphasized and what is omitted. The literature on the new Constitution – its origins, its content, its significance – has become voluminous, especially in Japanese.

forces have committed themselves to that end. In the final analysis that is what is significant and what counts.

What weaknesses did the SCAP authorities see in the Imperial Diet of the Meiji Constitution and what changes did they seek to incorporate in the draft constitution they prepared?[1] (1) In the Meiji Constitution, sovereignty resided in the Emperor. This was perceived as being in direct contravention to the doctrine of popular sovereignty, a doctrine they believed to be fundamental to a democratic political system. (2) The Imperial Diet was judged to have had no power over the budget. (3) The Imperial Diet was weak as its annual sessions lasted for only three months. They could be extended only by Imperial Order. (4) The Imperial Diet was subordinate to the imperial bureaucracy, which was the seat of real power. 'In short, the members of the [Imperial] Diet, within limits, were empowered by the Constitution to talk.'[2]

These perceived shortcomings of the Imperial Diet under the Meiji Constitution became the focal points for the sweeping institutional changes that SCAP introduced in the 1947 Constitution. First and foremost, though the Emperor was retained, his role was reduced to being 'the symbol of the State and the unity of the people, deriving his position from the will of the people with whom resides sovereign power.'[3] Second, the Diet became 'the highest organ of state power, and ... the sole law-making organ of the State'.[4] Third, the largely hereditary House of Peers was replaced by an elected House of Councillors. Fourth, the House of Representatives was accorded primacy in approving the budget and international treaties.[5] Fifth, executive power was vested in the Cabinet (all Ministers must be civilians) which was made responsible to the Diet.[6]

Merely to alter Constitutional norms would not necessarily change the actual *modus operandi* of the government. The authors of the policy guidelines in the American Government and the SCAP officials may have been optimists, but they were not fools. A veritable avalanche of directives flowed from SCAP to the Japanese Government, which was instructed to undertake a fundamental reordering of laws, atti-

---

[1]Much of this section is based on 'The National Diet', *PRJ*, Vol. I, pp. 145–85, and personal recollections.

[2]*PRJ*, Vol. I, p. 152.

[3]The 1947 Constitution, Chapter I, Article 1, Fujii, *The Constitution of Japan*, pp. 309–10.

[4]The 1947 Constitution, Chapter IV, Article 41, *ibid*, p. 314.

[5]The 1947 Constitution, Chapter IV, Articles 60 and 61, *ibid.*, pp. 316–17.

[6]The 1947 Constitution, Chapter V, Articles 65 and 66, *ibid.*, pp. 317–18.

tudes, behavior, customs and traditions. The Japanese Government was turned into an instrument for introducing revolutionary changes by peaceful means. That the results achieved did not always match expectations is hardly surprising. That some of the reforms have made a lasting impact on Japanese politics is undoubtedly a tribute to the Japanese people's marvelous capacity to adapt to changed circumstances as well as their ability to mold intended changes so that they conform to their own needs and requirements. I very much doubt that many of us who worked in SCAP in those heady days would have been willing to be convinced that the Constitution would last without formal amendment for ten, let alone twenty-five years.

The new Constitution and its provisions which enhanced the role of the National Diet came into force amidst a sea of change. A few of the many reform programs will be mentioned to provide at least some indication of the Occupation's immense efforts during its initial two and a half years. Among the first was instructing the Japanese Government to remove all restrictions on political, civil, and religious liberties.[1] This directive ordered the abrogation of politically restrictive pieces of legislation such as the Peace Preservation Law, and the release of all political prisoners. Its enforcement resulted in the dismantling of the elaborate structure of political oppression that had been created to enforce national conformity and allowed those individuals who had been imprisoned for opposing the war effort and the policies leading up to it to participate once again in the politics of their country. Leaders of the left-wing parties were the chief beneficiaries. Many Japanese Socialists and Communists — if they were not in exile — had been detained for having advocated actions that had been labeled 'dangerous'. Their return to active political life obviously altered the spectrum of ideas, policies and programs which could be prominently articulated.

A second directive ordered the removal and barring of undesirable personnel from public office, more commonly referred to as the Purge.[2] Its goals were to remove from positions of power and exclude from political influence categories of indivduals who were deemed to be inimical to the growth of democratic political processes. Two major groups were adversely affected: career military officers and leaders of

---

[1]'Removal of Restriction on Political, Civil, and Religious Liberties', 4 October 1945. *PRJ*, Vol. II, pp. 463—5.
[2]'Removal and Exclusion of Undesirable Personnel from Public Office', 4 January 1946. *PRJ*, Vol. II, pp. 482—8.

the Imperial Rule Assistance Association and its various subsidiaries constituted 95 percent of all purgees.[1]

Just as the 'Civil Liberties' directive freed political prisoners, so the Purge sought to bar their jailors from the exercise of political power. Both programs gave serious recognition to the role of political leadership as a factor influencing and effectuating the kinds of sociopolitical change which SCAP was seeking to foster prior to the 'reverse course'. Without them, Constitutional and institutional tinkering would merely have resulted in allowing old wine to be poured into new bottles. With them, Japan's political map underwent a rapid – if highly controversial and, due to the midstream shifts in SCAP policies, temporary – transformation.

SCAP also deemed that excessive concentrations of economic power were inimical to the growth of democracy. The SWNCC and JCS policy guidelines directed the dismantling of the industrial component of Japan's warmaking potential and the encouragement of 'wide distribution of income and of ownership of the means of production and trade' as well as the 'development of organizations in labor, industry, and agriculture organized on a democratic basis'.[2] The Occupation sought to achieve these policy goals through the implementation of several complex programs. Anti-monopoly legislation was enforced against the giant *zaibatsu* conglomerates. Encouragement was given to the growth of an effective trade union movement in industry. A far-reaching land reform succeeded in eliminating tenant farming with minor and inconsequential exceptions. Each of these added its increment to the controlled revolution, itself a possible contradiction in terms, that the Occupation initially tried to bring about.

This list of Occupation-sponsored reforms, which is only a selective sample, is to be viewed against the immense landscape of all the other programs that were undertaken. Both the institutional structure and the content of education, the media of information, religion, the family, the role of women – nothing was left untouched by the outpouring of SCAP directives, memoranda and suggestions. Admittedly, most of this reformist zeal was concentrated into the first three years of the Occupation. Furthermore, many of them did not really succeed in fulfilling the overblown claims of General MacArthur's public relations

---

[1]For further details, please see my *The Purge of Japanese Leaders*, p. 80 and *passim*.

[2]Joint Chiefs of Staff Directive, Part II, Paragraphs 25a and b, *PRJ*, Vol. II, p. 435.

specialists, some of whose efforts were designed to promote his candidacy for the Republican Party's presidential nomination in 1948.

What was amazing was the willingness of the Japanese people at that time to accept most of this relentless prodding with equanimity. There is no entirely satisfactory explanation for their behavior. Their defeat in war, their respect for the authority of those who had defeated them, their traditional acceptance of the vicissitudes of fate, undoubtedly provide partial clues, but they are incomplete and insufficient. Further inquiry is needed into the extent to which different segments of Japanese society had actually anticipated many of the SCAP reforms completely independently and were thus eager to support them, even though their sponsors were *gaijin* (foreigners) and most Japanese do not relish *gaijin* meddling in their internal affairs.[1] In the more recent past, this latter personality trait has become more and more evident; it is understandable if you take into account the changes that were forced on them by foreigners immediately after the Second World War.

This digression into related, but tangential, realms of Occupation policies and endeavors was not intended to provide an overview of this complex undertaking called the Allied Occupation of Japan. Rather, its purpose was to suggest that the creation of the National Diet should not be perceived as an isolated phenomenon or as an abstract exercise in administrative reorganization. Within the larger context the Diet was restructured and its internal rules of procedure were altered.

The creation of the Kokkai

Teikoku Gikai (Imperial Diet, the *'Gi'* means deliberation, the *'kai'* assembly) has been the official name of the parliament under the Meiji Constitution. This was changed to *Kokkai* (a combination of *'koku'* meaning nation or people and the same *'kai'*; the *'u'* in *'koku'* is elided when the component elements are pronounced together). It was hoped that more than a solely symbolic modification would eventuate.

---

[1]The literature on the Occupation era in Japanese politics is growing, but it is still woefully inadequate, especially from the Japanese perspective. Japanese scholarship on this topic only began seriously about five years ago, with the major exception being the work of the Constitution Investigation Commission. That era still touches — understandably enough — some raw and sensitive nerves, but less so than in the years when the Japanese people were struggling with the manifold problems of economic recovery.

SCAP officials and Members of the House of Representatives quickly recognized that it was not only the Meiji Constitution that had placed restraints on the Imperial Diet. It had also been hobbled by its internal rules and regulations: the Imperial Law of the Houses and its companion Ordinance concerning the House of Peers. Hence, while the new Constitution itself was still being discussed, the law regulating procedure in the as yet to be established House of Representatives and House of Councillors was being revised.

The new Diet Law[1] accomplished several purposes. First, it raised the status of the Members by placing their salaries on a par with those received by the highest ranking bureaucrats, the Administrative Vice-Ministers (*Jimu Jikan*, who are not to be confused with *Seimu Jikan*, the Parliamentary Vice-Ministers). Second, the budget for the Diet was placed under its control rather than that of the Finance Ministry. Third, each Member was given a private office and secretarial assistance as well as franking privileges and free passes on the national railroads in order to encourage communication with constituents. Fourth, the presiding officers of each chamber were to be elected by the Members rather than appointed by the Emperor as had been the case in the Imperial Diet. Fifth, a Diet Library patterned after the Library of Congress was established, as were legislative reference bureaus in each of the two Houses to provide assistance to Members in the drafting of bills. Sixth, an elaborate subject-matter committee system was created in each chamber (this subject will receive extended treatment in Chapter 3).

If some of this sounds familiar to anyone who has studied Congress' periodic efforts to reorganize itself, it should not be surprising. 'Government section of GHQ rendered every assistance throughout this period [of drafting the Diet Law], supplying us with the Legislative Reorganization Act of 1946 as passed by the United States Senate . . .'[2] This had its beneficial effects. Using the American Congress as a model provided those who worked on the Diet Law with an institution that still enjoyed great prestige and exercised power independent of the executive. However, this also created considerable confusion. American constitutional theory rests on the separation of powers doctrine. Whatever one may think about the efficacy of that doctrine in the American system of government, its utility for the Japanese

---

[1]Law No. 79, 19 March 1947, *PRJ*, Vol. II, pp. 968—76.
[2]Remarks of Oike Makoto, Chief Clerk (Director General) of the House of Representatives (Secretariat), 19 December 1946, as quoted in *PRJ*, Vol. I, p. 158.

Diet was highly questionable. After all, that institution exists within a parliamentary framework in which there is a fusion of executive and legislative power; the Cabinet (executive) is — at least formally — elected by the Diet and responsible to it. Hence, to base crucial provisions of the Diet Law (for example, the committee system) on the Congressional Legislative Reorganization Act, which rested on the presupposition that the Congress was an independent and coequal branch of government with the executive, was to pay inappropriate homage to American political doctrine.

The Diet Law also contains another curious dual set of features. On the one hand, presiding officers are given incredibly broad powers; they can call a plenary meeting on their own authority, they can fix the agenda, they can limit debate, and they can maintain order. Concurrently, Members are given minimal countervailing powers. If one-fifth of the Members protest the time limit set by the presiding officer, all he has to do is to submit the motion to the House and a simple majority can vote down the protestors. These provisions were written into the Diet Law 'so as to prevent filibustering'.[1] Once again, a feature of American Congressional practice, which as in this instance the SCAP advisors disliked, influenced the Diet's subsequent operations in entirely unanticipated ways.

It is one thing to have reservations about 'filibustering'. It has proved to be something completely different to have allowed that reservation to accord powers to the presiding officers with which they can — with the help of the majority — silence the minority. SCAP officials with great determination totally overlooked the many features of Congressional organization which give substantial powers to minority views; independent committees and even more independent committee chairmen, vast dispersal of authority over the agenda, the filibuster in the Senate, and the lack of party discipline in voting, to mention only the most obvious.

This is not to imply approval of these features of Congress, but to indicate some of the hazards involved in transferring one's likes and dislikes from one political system to another. One consequence of it all has been to reduce the Opposition to being nothing more than bystanders in the Diet's legislative process. That might have happened anyway, given the subsequent evolution of the Japanese political party system, but it is nonetheless surprising that the drafters of the Diet Law and their American advisors were so unconcerned about

[1] *PRJ*, Vol. I, p. 163.

protecting minority prerogatives. Like the *umeboshi* (a pickled plum), it leaves a bitter aftertaste.

Why was there this lack of concern with procedural safeguards for the minority or Opposition viewpoints? After all, many of my erstwhile associates in Government Section were liberals, and let me hasten to add I am not using the term pejoratively. Furthermore, several Government Section officials actively promoted the establishment of the Japanese Civil Liberties Union. It was not a lack of awareness of issues relating to minority rights or downright hostility towards them as was exhibited by certain career military officers who were in positions of responsibility inside SCAP. It was instead – as I desperately try to dredge up my own attitudes as well as those I heard expressed in those years – that all of us were predominantly goal-oriented. The SWNCC and JCS directives had to be carried out and speedily, because who knew how long the opportunity to effectuate all those reforms for the Japanese people would last? Secondly, many of these reform programs had to be translated into Japanese law – through the instrument of the Diet, of course. Any opposition to them would, in all probability, come from the Diet's more conservative sectors. Too many procedural safeguards would only give them the opportunity to delay the coming of the millennium. Some of this attitude does unintentionally surface in the passing reference to 'filibustering' in the officially approved history of the Diet in *Political Reorientation of Japan*. Additionally, no one in Government Section had worked in Congress. All who had had prior political or governmental experience had been with executive agencies, and carried with them the biases of executive prerogatives. It is all reminiscent of Montesquieu and his mistaken interpretation of the English system of government in the eighteenth century which led to the separation of powers doctrine as embodied in the American Constitution. Confusion of premises, misapplication of doctrine, combined with biases on behalf of executive power, were all propounded with zeal to the Japanese officials who dutifully incorporated it into the Diet Law. It was all done with the best of intentions and – I vouch for this – absolutely no malice.

Contrary to the lack of concern for the protection of minority viewpoints which becomes obvious when reading of the powers of the presiding officers, bicameralism was retained in the National Diet. There was some discussion by Government Section officials that the Diet under the new Constitution should only have a single chamber. The idea of a unicameral legislature was toyed with but never received wide support.'[1] To have accepted that alternative was considered too radical a departure from tradition. Furthermore, it was thought that an irresponsible majority might capture control of the lower house, and an upper house — if there were one — could act as a brake. On the other hand, the existing House of Peers, by virtue of its aristocratic character and its excessively close relationship to the imperial institution, simply could not be retained without doing serious violence to the democratization of Japanese politics. Out of this welter of conflicting concerns emerged plans for the House of Councillors.

The *Sangi-in*, as the House of Councillors is called in Japanese, is not really an 'upper house', although that designation is frequently used in referring to it. Constitutionally, the House of Councillors shares several important powers with the House of Representatives. First, any Constitutional Amendment must be initiated by a 'concurring vote of two-thirds of all members of each house'.[2] Second, the Cabinet is responsible to the Diet, not just the House of Representatives,[3] but in the selection of the Prime Minister it is the House of Representatives' decision which prevails in case there is a disagreement between the two chambers.[4] Third, both Houses share the legislative power except with respect to the budget and treaty approval, in which fields the decisions of the House of Representatives prevail (more of this topic later); moreover, the Representatives can override the Councillors with a two-thirds majority of the members present.[5]

The House of Councillors is also accorded one unique role. 'When the House of Representatives is dissolved [prior to holding an election], the House of Councillors is closed at the same time. However, the Cabinet may in time of national emergency convoke the House of

---

[1]*PRJ*, Vol. I, p. 108. This is stated as if the discussion took place among the Japanese preparers of the Cabinet draft. It is my recollection that the decision to retain a second chamber had been made in Government Section at the time that the initial SCAP draft was being prepared. I was not in Government Section in February 1946 when the quasi-constitutional convention did most of its work, but that episode was still a lively topic of conversation among the staff when I joined it in October of the same year.

[2]The 1947 Constitution, Chapter IX, Article 96, Paragraph 1, Fujii, *The Constitution of Japan*, p. 322.

[3]The 1947 Constitution, Chapter V, Article 66, Paragraph 3, *ibid.*, p. 318.

[4]The 1947 Constitution, Chapter V, Article 67, Paragraph 2, *ibid.*, p. 318.

[5]The 1947 Constitution, Chapter IV, Articles 59, 60, 61, *ibid.*, pp. 316–17.

Councillors in emergency session'.[1] No occasion has yet occurred for this provision to be invoked; it is therefore not clear just exactly what the Councillors would actually accomplish after they had gathered together. This provision does reinforce one important point, however; the Councillors provide for continuity. They are elected for six-year terms, with only half of them facing election every three years. The House of Councillors cannot be dissolved. By contrast, the maximum term for Representatives between elections is four years, and there is always the prospect that the Prime Minister will call for an earlier election by dissolving the House, or if the Representatives pass a no-confidence resolution against the Cabinet.[2] Elections for the House of Representatives have been called for on the average of every two-and-a-half years, but only twice after a vote of no-confidence (in 1948 and 1953), and never formally since the conservatives united in the LDP in 1955.

The Councillors may be nearly equal to the Representatives in terms of the allocation of powers under the 1947 Constitution, but they are in an inferior position politically. That is why so much of the rest of this study will concentrate on the House of Representatives, with only occasional references to the House of Councillors. A few examples will underscore the relative positions of the two Houses. None of the Prime Ministers have been Councillors. Among Cabinet Ministers, only an average of three have come to be accorded to Councillors in each reorganization, with the balance of them (fifteen to seventeen) being Representatives. As noted, the Representatives are pre-eminent with respect to the Diet's approval of the Government's Budget and international treaties.

One other factor which has thus far been of great significance is that, by and large, the same political forces have controlled both Houses. This was not true in the first three elections for the House of Councillors (1947, 1950, and 1953) in which a substantial percentage of the elected Councillors were Independents, whose ideological allegiances were inconstant. However, it has very definitely been the case since the 1956 election, in which the previously disunited conservative Liberals and Democratic-Progressives ran under the united Liberal-Democratic Party label for the first time.

As is made clear by Table 1, Councillors are elected in two kinds of

---

[1] The 1947 Constitution, Chapter IV, Article 54, *ibid.*, pp. 315–16.
[2] The 1947 Constitution, Chapter V, Article 69, *ibid.*, p. 318.

constituencies. Out of the total of 252,[1] 100 are elected in the nation-wide constituency, with each voter casting his vote for only one candidate; the others are elected in Prefecturewide constituencies, originally apportioned to reflect the uneven distribution of population so that heavily populated Tokyo received eight seats, while Prefectures with smaller populations were accorded a minimum of two, and with each voter again casting his ballot for only one candidate.[2] (Prefectures are administrative sub-divisions of Japan which are something of a hybrid between French Departments and American States.) At a minimum, this is a peculiar electoral system and reflects the many compromises that were made among Government Section and Japanese Government officials. In its defense, it is important to note that it preserves the principle of public election in contrast to some of the proposals which were based on variations of appointive techniques.

Inevitably, some strange results have been obtained in House of Councillors elections, despite their general similarity with those for the House of Representatives. The nationwide constituency has been advantageous to candidates with large personal followings such as the novelist Ishihara Shintarō, who gained the largest personal vote in the 1971 Councillors' election, over three million, with his nearest competitor, Aoshima Yukio, a television 'tarento' (talent), picking up only 1,200,000.[3] Population shifts have also taken their toll in badly skewing the results. In the same election, for example, a Communist lost in Tokyo while picking up nearly 640,000 votes, but in neighboring Chiba Prefecture, a Liberal-Democrat (conservative) was victorious with only 270,000 votes. Even worse disparities can be found.[4]

All this was to have been expected in a system which at least partially duplicates the disparate ratios of population to individual Senators in the American Congress. In this connection one additional feature of Senatorial elections was copied. In all of the elections except the first, in which all new Councillors were elected, only half of the total (plus any vacancies) are elected every three years. This staggering of terms allows for structural continuity in the House of Councillors; although

---

[1]Originally there were 250 seats, but two new ones were added at the time of Okinawa's reversion to Japan in 1972.
[2]'The Law for the Election of Members of the House of Councillors', *PRJ*, Vol. II, pp. 852–63.
[3]*Kokkai Binran* [Diet Handbook] (Tokyo: Nihon Seikei Shimbunsha, August 1972), p. 320.
[4]*Ibid.*, pp. 316–17.

Table 1 *House of Councillors election results: seats won*

Election	Constituency	Party		Ryokufu Green (Breeze Society)	Minor
		Liberal	Democratic-Progressive		
1st: 1947	National	8 (8.0)	6 (6.0)	—	9 (9.0)
	Local	30 (20.0)	22 (14.6)	—	13 (8.7)
	Total	38 (15.2)	28 (11.2)	—	22 (8.8)
2nd: 1950	N	18 (32.1)	1 (1.8)	6 (10.7)	2 (3.6)
	L	34 (44.8)	8 (10.5)	3 (3.9)	3 (3.9)
	T	52 (39.4)	9 (6.8)	9 (6.8)	5 (3.8)
3rd: 1953	N	16 (30.1)	3 (5.7)	8 (15.1)	—
	L	30 (40.0)	5 (6.7)	8 (10.7)	1 (1.3)
	T	46 (35.9)	8 (6.3)	16 (12.5)	1 (0.8)
4th: 1956	N	Liberal-Democratic 19 (36.5)		5 (9.6)	1 (2.0)
	L	42 (56.0)		—	—
	T	61 (55.9)		5 (3.9)	1 (0.8)

			Dōshi (Friends)	
5th: 1959	N	22 (42.3)	4 (7.7)	1 (1.9)
	L	49 (65.3)	2 (2.7)	— —
	T	71 (55.9)	6 (4.7)	1 (0.8)
6th: 1962	N	21 (41.2)	2 (3.9)	
	L	48 (63.3)	—	
	T	69 (54.3)	2 (1.6)	
7th: 1965	N	25 (48.2)		
	L	46 (61.4)		
	T	71 (55.9)		
8th: 1968	N	21 (41.2)		
	L	48 (64.0)		
	T	69 (54.7)		
9th: 1971	N	21 (42.0)		
	L	42 (55.4)		
	T	63 (50.0)		

Source: Nishihira Shigeki, *Nihon No Senkyō* [Japan's Elections] (Tokyo: Shiseido, 1972), pp. 270–1.

Table 1 continued

Election	Independent	Party		Communist	Total
		Socialist			
1st: 1947	57 (57.0)	17 (17.0)		3 (3.0)	100
	54 (36.0)	30 (20.0)		1 (0.7)	150
	111 (44.4)	47 (18.8)		4 (1.6)	250
2nd: 1950	12 (21.4)	15 (26.8)		2 (3.6)	56
	7 (9.2)	21 (27.7)		—	76
	19 (14.4)	36 (27.3)		2 (1.5)	132
		Right JSP	Left JSP		
3rd: 1953	15 (28.3)	3 (5.7)	8 (15.1)	—	53
	14 (18.7)	7 (9.3)	10 (13.3)	—	75
	29 (22.7)	10 (7.8)	18 (14.0)	—	128
		Socialist			
4th: 1956	5 (9.6)	21 (40.3)		1 (2.0)	52
	4 (5.4)	28 (37.3)		1 (1.3)	75
	9 (7.1)	49 (38.6)		2 (1.6)	127

		Komei Political League	Democratic-Socialist	Socialist		
5th: 1959	7 (13.5)			17 (32.7)	1 (1.9)	52
	3 (4.0)			21 (28.0)	—	75
	10 (7.9)			38 (29.9)	1 (0.8)	127
6th: 1962	1 (2.0)	7 (13.7)	3 (5.9)	15 (29.4)	2 (3.9)	51
	2 (2.6)	2 (2.6)	1 (1.3)	22 (28.9)	1 (1.3)	76
	3 (2.2)	9 (7.3)	4 (3.2)	37 (29.2)	3 (2.2)	127
		Kōmeitō				
7th: 1965	2 (3.8)	9 (17.3)	2 (3.8)	12 (23.1)	2 (3.8)	52
	1 (1.3)	2 (2.7)	1 (1.3)	24 (32.0)	1 (1.3)	75
	3 (2.4)	11 (8.6)	3 (2.4)	36 (28.3)	3 (2.4)	127
8th: 1968	2 (3.9)	9 (17.7)	4 (7.8)	12 (23.5)	3 (5.9)	51
	3 (4.0)	4 (5.3)	3 (4.0)	16 (21.4)	1 (1.3)	75
	5 (4.0)	13 (10.3)	7 (5.6)	28 (22.2)	4 (3.2)	126
9th: 1971	1 (2.0)	8 (16.0)	4 (8.0)	11 (22.0)	5 (10.0)	50
	1 (1.3)	2 (2.6)	2 (2.6)	28 (36.8)	1 (1.3)	76
	2 (1.6)	10 (7.9)	6 (4.8)	39 (30.9)	6 (4.8)	126

Table 2 *House of Councillors election results: popular vote (%) in '000s'*

Election	Constituency	Party			
		Liberal	Democratic	Ryokufu (Green Breeze Society)	Independent
1st: 1947	National	1,360 (6.4)	1,508 (7.1)		12,699 (59.7)
	Local	3,770 (17.1)	2,989 (13.6)		7,527 (34.1)
2nd: 1950	N	Hatoyama Liberal 111 (0.4) Yoshida Liberal 8,314 (29.7)	People's Democratic 1,369 (4.9)	3,660 (13.1)	7,633 (27.3)
	L	Hatoyama Liberal 523 (1.9) Yoshida Liberal 10,415 (35.9)	2,966 (10.2)	1,774 (6.1)	3,466 (12.0)
3rd: 1953	N	6,150 (22.8)	Progressive 1,631 (6.0)	3,301 (12.2)	9,504 (35.2)
	L	3,803 (31.4)	2,840 (10.1)	2,096 (7.5)	6,013 (21.5)

		Liberal-Democratic	Dōshi (Friends)	
4th: 1956	N	11,357 (39.7)	2,877 (10.1)	4,444 (15.5)
	L	14,354 (48.4)	654 (2.2)	2,136 (7.1)
5th: 1959	N	12,121 (41.2)	2,383 (8.1)	5,817 (19.8)
	L	15,667 (52.0)	731 (2.4)	2,311 (7.7)
6th: 1962	N	16,582 (46.4)	1,660 (4.7)	1,404 (3.9)
	L	17,113 (47.1)	129 (0.4)	1,726 (4.8)
7th: 1965	N	17,583 (47.2)		1,701 (4.6)
	L	16,651 (44.2)		1,665 (4.4)
8th: 1968	N	20,120 (46.7)		2,872 (6.7)
	L	19,406 (44.9)		1,910 (4.4)
9th: 1971	N	17,759 (44.4)		2,343 (5.9)
	L	17,915 (44.0)		1,916 (4.7)

Adapted from: Nishihira, *Nihon No Senkyō* [Japan's Elections], pp. 266—7.

Table 2 continued

Election	Minor Parties		Socialist		JCP		Total
1st: 1947	1,613	(7.6)	3,480	(16.3)	611	(2.9)	21,271
	2,037	(9.2)	4,901	(22.2)	825	(3.8)	22,049
2nd: 1950	829	(2.9)	4,855	(17.3)	1,334	(4.8)	27,999
	1,430	(4.9)	7,317	(25.2)	1,637	(5.7)	29,005
3rd: 1953			Right JSP	Left JSP			
	445	(1.6)	1,740 (6.4)	3,859 (14.3)	294	(1.1)	27,035
	600	(2.2)	2,953 (10.5)	3,918 (14.0)	265	(0.9)	28,011
4th: 1956			Socialist				
	789	(2.7)	8,550	(29.9)	599	(2.1)	28,616
	236	(0.8)	11,156	(37.6)	1,149	(3.9)	29,686

		Komei Political League / Komeitō	DSP	JSP		
5th: 1959	753 (2.5)			7,795 (26.5)	552 (1.9)	29,420
	155 (0.5)			10,265 (34.1)	999 (3.3)	30,129
6th: 1962	296 (0.8)	4,124 (11.5)	1,900 (5.3)	8,667 (24.3)	1,124 (3.1)	35,757
	59 (0.2)	958 (2.6)	2,649 (7.3)	11,918 (32.8)	1,760 (4.8)	36,312
7th: 1965	298 (0.8)	5,098 (13.7)	2,214 (5.9)	8,730 (23.4)	1,652 (4.2)	37,277
	186 (0.5)	1,911 (5.1)	2,304 (6.1)	12,347 (32.8)	2,609 (6.9)	37,672
8th: 1968	158 (0.4)	6,657 (15.4)	2,579 (6.0)	8,542 (19.8)	2,147 (5.0)	43,074
	107 (0.2)	2,633 (6.1)	3,010 (6.9)	12,618 (29.2)	3,577 (8.3)	43,260
9th: 1971	48 (0.1)	5,626 (14.1)	2,442 (6.1)	8,494 (21.3)	3,219 (8.1)	39,932
	77 (0.2)	1,392 (4.7)	1,920 (3.4)	12,598 (31.0)	4,879 (12.0)	40,697

this factor has not been as significant as might have been anticipated. There is also substantial continuity in the membership of the House of Representatives due to the extremely high percentage of incumbents that are re-elected.

In one crucial respect the creators of the House of Councillors as an institution and of its electoral system may have accomplished more than they could reasonably be expected to have anticipated. 'The two bodies [House of Representatives and House of Councillors] are chosen by different methods in order that all interests may be effectively represented and in order that one house may act as a check or modifying influence on the other.'[1] In this respect, the framers of the Constitution did bring the principle of limiting the powers of the majority to bear on their work. Thus far, this expectation has not been fulfilled for the simple and obvious reason that the same set of political forces has controlled working majorities in both chambers. Hence, what is done in one chamber is duplicated in the other. Conceivably, this situation could change in the none too distant future.

Subsequent to the House of Councillors election in 1971, the distribution of party strengths was as shown in Table 3.

One way of looking at this distribution of seats is to add the three 'Independents' to the total held by the Liberal-Democrats. This would be reasonable because they include the President and Vice-President of the House of Councillors, both of whom are believed to be likely to vote with the Liberal-Democrats. (See pp. 77—78.) Assuming for the

Table 3[2]   *Distribution of party strengths in House of Councillors (1973)*

Party	No. of Seats
Liberal-Democratic	134
Japan Socialist	65
Komeitō	23
Democratic-Socialist	13
Japan Communist	10
2nd Chambers (*Ni-in*) Club	4
Independents	3
Total	252

[1]*PRJ*, Vol. I, p. 185.
[2]*Kokkai Binran*, p. 84.

moment that the Members of the '2nd Chamber Club' (*Ni-In Kurabu*) would vote with the Opposition parties (Socialists, Komeitō, Democratic-Socialists, Communists), their total strength is 115, by contrast with the 137 for the Government side. A shift of twelve seats — a prospect that cannot be ruled out as being impossible — would provide the combined Opposition forces with control over the House of Councillors.

In that event the function of the House of Councillors, of being a 'check or modifying influence' on the House of Representatives, would receive its first real test. Until this actually happens it is difficult to predict its impact on the operations of the Diet. One thing is clear. In the interim the House of Councillors will remain what it has been thus far: a pale carbon-copy of the House of Representatives.

The National Diet has been in existence since 1947. It inherited certain legacies from the Imperial Diet. First, an impressive building in the heart of Tokyo continued to be its home. Second, like its predecessor, it is a bicameral legislative body; but unlike its predecessor, both Houses are popularly elected.

But external appearances apart the National Diet was a very different institution — in Constitutional theory at least — from its prewar namesake. It was to be the 'highest organ of state power, and . . . the sole law-making organ of the State'. At the time of its birth, the Occupation was still imbued with a missionary-like reformist zeal which was matched by a Japanese Government that was in the hands of the only Socialist ever to have become Prime Minister, the mild Katayama Tetsu. In the context of the times, it was an auspicious beginning; but the fundamental question still remained: could the Diet live up to its new mandate?

CHAPTER TWO

Parties, factions and the Diet

In the byways of Tokyo's Akasaka district just down the hill from the Diet Buildiing are to be found numerous *ryotei*, a term which is inadequately translated as 'Restaurants'. Delicious food is served, and possibly far more importantly private rooms are provided for discreet conversations among Japan's political elite. In the last quarter century a sprinkling of political party leaders has always been included; it was not always so. In prewar Japan, effective power was in the hands of higher-class civilian bureaucrats (*bucho* — section chief upwards), corporation executives and senior echelons of the military. Today, the civilian bureaucracy may still constitute Japan's governing class, but it is the political party leaders who rule. Lest it be forgotten, the Diet is the instrument through which these politicians exercise their power.

Japan's political party system has undergone a number of transformations since the end of the Pacific War. In the immediate aftermath of defeat, a multi-party system emerged. There were two major conservative parties which adopted the names 'Liberal' and 'Progressive' (also 'Democratic') and were the descendants of the prewar Seiyukai and Minseito respectively. Around the center of the ideological spectrum a number of minor parties emerged, of which the most significant was the 'Cooperative Party' (later called the 'People's Cooperative Party') under the leadership of Miki Takeo. He and his followers ultimately joined the conservatives. The Japan Socialist Party quickly established itself as the major left-wing force by bringing together various strands of the prewar non-Communist left. In addition to the Japan Communist Party, which for the first time was accorded legal status, a large number of splinter parties ran a substantial number of candidates (most of whom were unsuccessful) in the three elections held under the Occupation (1946, 1947, and 1949). Of these, only the Communists established a foothold, but one which they soon lost. It took more than twenty years for them to recover and to become a national party again.

This multi-party structure lasted until 1955 when, during a banner year, the conservatives merged into a unified Liberal-Democratic Party

(LDP) six months after the Socialists (who had split into 'Right' and 'Left' parties) in 1951 had reunited. Japan's political party system seemed to be evolving into a relatively stable two-party structure during the last half of the 1950s. Power, as measured in number of seats in the Diet, was notably unequal between the two parties, with the LDP coming close to winning two-thirds and the Socialist not quite one-third of the seats, the remainder going to a small offshoot of the JSP and to the Communists. It was, as Scalapino and Masumi have pointed out, more properly labeled a one-and-a-half party system.[1]

A new and far more permanent split in the Socialist Party — from which the Democratic-Socialist Party under Nishio Suehiro emerged as a separate entity — ushered in the 1960s. The Sōka-Gakkai, a neo-Buddhist religious group spawned Komeitō (Clean Government Party), that carved out a distinctive but ideologically imprecise niche for itself by the middle of the decade. In the interim, the Communist Party had been slowly and painfully rehabilitating itself from the debacles of Cominform criticism and the 'Red' Purge as a force in Japanese politics. These efforts paid off handsomely in the December 1972 House of Representatives election, when it won the largest number of seats ever (39 plus one 'Independent'), thereby surpassing both the Komeitō and the Democratic-Socialists. These developments did not alter the basic shape of Japan's party system, however. As has been the case for nearly the entire postwar period, and most definitely so since 1955, the conservatives in the LDP held a preponderant share of power and the Opposition was, by comparison, weak and fragmented. Table 4 gives a detailed overview.

Japanese newspapers tend to classify the voting public into two major groupings, the *hoshu-kei* ('conservative group') and the *kakushin-kei* ('progressive' or 'reformist group'). Election results provide a somewhat different picture when viewed from this perspective rather than from one based entirely on the strengths of the various parties in the Diet. While it is virtually impossible to be completely precise about the popular vote classification in the immediate postwar years because of the multiplicity of minor parties and the large number of 'Independents' who ran, it is reasonable to assert that the popular vote supporting conservative candidates did not fall below 60% of the total, and in several elections (1949, 1952, 1953 and

---

[1]Robert A. Scalapino and Masumi Junnosuke, *Parties and Politics in Contemporary Japan* (Berkeley and Los Angeles: University of California Press, 1962) .

Table 4 *House of Representatives election results: seats won*

Election year	Liberal	Party Progressive (Shimpō)	Cooperative	Independent	Minor Parties
22nd: 1946	140 (30,2)	94 (20,3)	14 (3,0)	81 (17,4)	38 (8,2)
23rd: 1947	131 (28,1)	Democratic (Minshū) 121 (26,0)	People's Coop. 29 (6,2)	13 (2,8)	25 (5,4)
24th: 1949	Democratic-Liberal 264 (56,7)	69 (14,8)	14 (3,0)	12 (2,6)	17 (3,6)
25th: 1952	Liberal 240 (51,5)	Progressive 85 (18,2)		19 (4,1)	7 (1,5)

26th: 1953	Yoshida	Hatoyama			11 (2.4)	1 (0.2)
	199 (42.7)	35 (7.5)				
27th: 1955	Liberal	Democratic			6 (1.3)	2 (0.4)
	112 (24.0)	185 (39.6)				
28th: 1958	Democratic-Liberal				12 (2.6)	1 (0.2)
	287 (61.5)					
29th: 1960	296 (63.4)				5 (1.1)	1 (0.2)
30th: 1963	283 (60.6)				12 (2.6)	
31st: 1967	277 (57.0)				9 (1.9)	
32nd: 1969	288 (59.2)				16 (3.2)	
33rd: 1972*	271 (55.2)				14 (2.8)	2 (0.4)

Adapted from: Nishihira, *Nihon No Senkyō* [Japan's Elections] and *Asahi Shimbun*, 12 December 1972.

Table 4 continued

Election year	Party				Total
	Socialist		Labor-Farmer	Communist	
22nd: 1946	92 (19.8)			5 (1.1)	464
23rd: 1947	143 (30.7)			4 (0.8)	466
24th: 1949	48 (10.3)		7 (1.5)	35 (7.5)	466
	Right Soc.	Left Soc.			
25th: 1952	57 (12.2)	54 (11.6)	4 (0.9)	0 (0)	466
26th: 1953	66 (14.2)	72 (15.4)	5 (1.1)	1 (0.2)	466
27th: 1955	67 (14.3)	89 (19.1)	4 (0.9)	2 (0.4)	467

Socialist ←

34

	Komeitō	Democratic-Socialist	Socialist		
28th: 1958			166 (35.5)	1 (0.2)	467
29th: 1960		17 (3.7)	145 (31.0)	3 (0.6)	467
30th: 1963		23 (4.9)	144 (30.8)	5 (1.1)	467
31st: 1967	25 (5.1)	30 (6.2)	140 (28.8)	5 (1.0)	486
32nd: 1969	47 (9.9)	31 (6.3)	90 (18.5)	14 (2.9)	486
33rd: 1972*	29 (5.9)	19 (3.9)	118 (24.0)	38 (7.7)	491

Table 5 *House of Representatives election results: popular vote (in '000s)*

Election year	Party			
	Progressive	Liberal	Cooperative	Independent
22nd: 1946	10,351 (18.7)	13,506 (24.4)	1,800 (32)	11,325 (20.4)
23rd: 1947	Democratic 6,840 (25.0)	7,356 (26.9)	People's Coop. 1,916 (7.0)	1,581 (5.8)
24th: 1949	4,798 (15.7)	Democratic-Liberal 13,420 (43.9)	1,042 (3.4)	2,008 (6.6)
25th: 1952	Progressive 6,429 (18.2)	Liberal 16,938 (47.9)		2,355 (6.7)
26th: 1953	Hatoyama Liberal 3,055 (8.8) — 6,186 (17.9)	Yoshida Liberal 13,476 (39.0)		1,524 (4.4)

	Democratic	Liberal	Liberal-Democratic	
27th: 1955	13,536 (36.6)	9,849 (26.6)		1,229 (3.3)
28th: 1958			22,977 (57.8)	2,381 (6.0)
29th: 1960			22,740 (57.56)	1,119 (2.83)
30th: 1963			22,424 (54 67)	1,956 (4.77)
31st: 1967			22,448 (48.8)	2,554 (5.55)
32nd: 1969			22,382 (47,63)	2,493 (5,30)
33rd: 1972			24,563 (46.8)	2,646 (5.05)

Table 5 continued

Election year	Minor Parties	Party		Labor-Farmer	Communist	Total
		Socialist				
22nd: 1946	6,473 (11.7)	9,858 (17.8)		→	2,136 (3.8)	55,449
23rd: 1947	1,490 (5.4)	7,176 (26.2)			1,003 (3.7)	27,362
24th: 1949	1,602 (5.2)	4,130 (13.5)		607 (2.0)	2,985 (9.7)	30,593
25th: 1952	949 (2.7)	Right JSP 4,108 (11.6)	Left JSP 3,399 (9.6)	261 (0.7)	(897) (2.6)	35,337
26th: 1953	152 (0.4)	4,678 (13.5)	4,517 (13.1)	359 (1.0)	656 (1.9)	34,602

Election		Komeitō	Democratic-Socialist	Socialist			Total
27th: 1955	497 (1.3)		5,130 (13.9)	5,683 (15.3)	358 (1.0)	733 (2.0)	37,015
28th: 1958	288 (0.7)			Socialist 13,094 (32.9)		1,012 (2.6)	39,752
29th: 1960	142 (0.35)		3,464 (8.77)	10,887 (27.56)		1,157 (2.93)	39,509
30th: 1963	60 (0.15)		3,023 (7.37)	11,907 (29.03)		1,646 (4.01)	41,017
31st: 1967	101 (0.22)	2,472 (5.38)	3,404 (7.40)	12,826 (27.89)		2,791 (4.76)	45,997
32nd: 1969	81 (0.17)	5,125 (10.91)	3,637 (7.74)	10,074 (21.44)		3,199 (6.81)	46,990
33rd: 1972	143 (0.27)	4,437 (8.5)	3,661 (7.0)	11,479 (21.9)		5,497 (10.49)	52,425

Note: ( ) = % of Popular vote. Sources: Nishihira *Nihon No Senkyō* [Japan's Elections] p. 265 and

Asahi Shimbun. 12, December 1972.

1955) exceeded 65%. Since then there has been a steady, if un-spectacular, decline in the percentage of conservative voters. Thus, in the 1967 election for the House of Representatives, LDP candidates for the first time collected less than 50% (offset by the votes cast for conservative candidates running without the benefit of official LDP endorsement, that is, running as Independents and aligning themselves with the LDP after the election), and in 1972 the popular vote cast for progressive candidates actually exceeded that cast for conservatives, excluding Independents.

These trends in the popular vote have been somewhat obscured by the LDP leadership's superior tactical abilities. For example, in the 1969 election the LDP won 59.2% of the seats in the House of Representatives with only 47.6% of the popular vote and 55.2% of the seats with 46.6% of the vote in 1972. Achieving these results, given the vagaries of Japan's medium-sized multiple-member constituency system (which will be discussed in detail below), places a premium on a party's capacity to endorse just the right number of candidates and to organize the voters in each district to support the party's en-dorsees in an even-handed fashion. Obviously, the LDP has been more adept at this than the 'progressive' parties, in part because the latter contains a multiplicity of parties, not just warring factions as is the case in the LDP (though the JSP too suffers from this kind of intramural strife), and in part because the population shift from county to city has resulted in substantial — and growing — disparities in the size of electoral districts. The latter factor has increased the voting strength of the rural and semi-rural voters, who tend to support the LDP, at the expense of the urban voters, who are more likely to support Opposition party candidates. For example, in Chiba's 1st district, which has become one of Tokyo's suburbs, an Opposition (Komeitō) candidate lost despite receiving 140,622 votes while in Chiba's more rural 2nd district an Independent (LDP) candidate was elected with only 41,488 votes in the 1972 election. So long as the LDP manages to win more than 50% of the seats in the House of Representatives it is unlikely that a rapid adjustment of this kind of disparity can be anticipated; it is the Diet which controls amendments to the existing electoral law. Thus far the judiciary has avoided the issue by means of the political question formula.

An unevenly-shaped tripod supports the LDP. Financiers and indus-trialists provide financial support, either directly or through such organizations as the Keidanren (Federation of Economic Organizations), Nikkeiren (Japan Federation of Employers' Organizations), and Keizai Doyukai (Committee for Economic Development). Farmers, fishermen, white-collar workers and junior executives make up the core of the *kōen-kai* ('supporters' societies') which provide the votes. The bureaucracy provides policy and legislative guidance, and also serves as an incubator for LDP candidates. Each leg of this tripod is important and serves a dual function; each is a prop, and the hollow interior of each serves as a pipe through which demands are sent up to the leadership. It must be understood that these demands, or signals, are often contradictory. Finance Ministry bureaucrats may promote trade liberalization as a means of coping with balance of trade surpluses, and thereby possibly offsetting the need for yen revaluation, while Ministry of International Trade and Industry bureaucrats may contend that such a cure is worse than the disease. What is important is that these groups with demands who serve as props and thus have access to the pipe-lines have more influence upon the councils of the LDP than those who do not.

The Socialist and Democratic-Socialist parties have trade union federations as the bases of their organizational and voting strength. Sōhyō (General Council of Japanese Trade Unions) does for the JSP what Domei Kaigi (Japan Confederation of Labor) does less successfully for the DSP. Endless debates take place in both parties and the union federations with which they are affiliated concerning the advantages and disadvantages of their dependence. While neither seems willing or able to cut the mutually beneficial umbilical cords, it goes without saying that these ties also impose constraints. For the political parties, it means that ideological orientations of the union leadership must be respected even if doing so might limit the pool of potential supporters. For the unions, it means that their influence over public policy remains relatively negligible so long as the parties with which they are affiliated are parts of a permanent Opposition. Most important, it means that the trade union movement has considerably less influence in the policy-making process than the size of the trade union electorate would appear to warrant.

Both the JSP and DSP are finding themselves challenged with increasing vigor by the rejuvenated Communist Party (JCP). The gains posted by the JCP over the last three House of Representative elections (from 5 seats in 1967 to 14 in 1949 to 39 in 1972) have been impressive and somewhat unanticipated. The JCP has the advantage of relying on its own organizational capabilities and its own fund-raising efforts

Table 6 *House of Representatives election results*

Election	Liberal	Progr.	Coop.	Ind.	Minor Parties	Socialist	Labor-Farmer	JCP
22nd: 1946 A.	24.4	18.7	3.2	20.4	11.7	17.8		3.8
B.	30.2	20.3	3.0	17.4	8.2	19.8		1.1
23rd: 1947 A.	26.9	Democ. 25.0	7.0	5.8	5.4	26.2		3.7
B.	28.1	26.0	6.2	2.8	5.4	30.7		0.8
24th 1949 A.	Democ-Liberal 43.9	15.7	3.4	6.6	5.2	13.5	2.0	9.7
B.	56.7	14.8	3.0	2.6	3.6	10.3	1.5	7.5
25th: 1952 A.	Liberal 47.9	Progressive 18.2		6.7	2.7	Right JSP 11.6 / Left JSP 9.6	0.7	2.6
B.	51.5	18.2		4.1	1.5	Right JSP 12.2 / Left JSP 11.6	0.9	0
26th: 1953 A.	Yoshida Lib. 39.0 / Hatoyama Lib. 8.8	Progressive 17.9		4.4	0.4	Right JSP 13.5 / Left JSP 13.1	1.0	1.9
B.	42.7 / 7.5	16.3		2.4	0.2	Right JSP 14.2 / Left JSP 15.4	1.1	0.2

		Liberal	Democratic	Liberal-Democratic			Komeitō	Democ. Soc.	Socialist		
27th: 1955	A.	26.6	36.6		3.3	1.3		13.9	15.3	1.0	2.0
	B.	24.0	39.6		1.3	0.4		14.3	19.1	0.9	0.4
28th: 1958	A.			57.8	6.0	0.7			32.9		2.6
	B.			61.5	2.6	0.2			35.5		0.2
29th: 1960	A.			57.6	2.8	0.4		8.8	27.6		2.9
	B.			63.4	1.1	0.2		3.7	31.0		0.6
30th: 1963	A.			54.7	4.8	0.15		7.4	29.0		4.0
	B.			60.6	2.6	—		4.9	30.8		1.1
31st: 1967	A.			48.8	5.6	0.22	5.4	7.4	27.9		4.8
	B.			57.0	1.9	—	5.1	6.2	28.8		1.0
32nd: 1969	A.			47.6	5.3	0.17	10.9	7.7	21.4		6.8
	B.			59.2	3.2	—	9.9	6.3	18.5		2.9
33rd: 1972	A.			46.8	5.0	0.3	8.5	7.0	21.9		10.5
	B.			55.2	2.8	0.4	5.9	3.9	24.0		7.7

Source: Based on Tables 4 and 5. A. % of popular vote. B. Seats won.

instead of the trade union federations. It also has expended far more energy than the JSP in tackling the problems of daily life, and far less on ideological debate.

Last, but by no means least of the Opposition parties is the Komeitō, the only genuinely new party in postwar Japan, as all of the others can trace their roots back to the prewar period. Its basic appeal has been to that segment of the Japanese public which migrated into the major urban centers in the economic boom years of the 1950s and 1960s and could not cope with the new surroundings. Originally it was the political handmaiden of the neo-Buddhist Sōka-Gakkai (Value-Creation Society), but the Komeitō's current relationship with this body is ambiguous. Formally, the two organization have severed the bonds which united them, but how complete the break is remains in question. The Komeitō's fortunes sagged in the December 1972 election for a number of reasons. Undoubtedly, the aftermath of the separation from the parent body played a role; so did a series of well-publicized, particularly by the JCP, scandals involving alleged interference with freedom of the press; also its fuzzy ideological image together with its seeming vacillation *vis-à-vis* the LDP contributed to voter disenchantment. Additionally, its candidates who were faced with Communist opponents did not fare well in several urban districts. It remains to be seen whether it is the Komeitō or the JCP which has been the proverbial flash in the pan.

Certain other aspects of the Japanese political party system require some elaboration to understand the behavior of their representatives in both chambers of the Diet. First, and possibly foremost, a deep and seemingly irreconcilable ideological chasm has persisted between the conservatives and progressive 'houses' for the greater part of the postwar period. This chasm was particularly evident with respect to foreign policy problems such as the alliance with the United States — conservatives generally in favor of it, progressives generally opposed — or policy towards China — until the summer of 1972 the conservatives had generally supported the maintenance of official ties with Taiwan, whereas the progressives had tended to favor early establishment of official diplomatic relations with the People's Republic of China. There were also profound differences over perennial domestic issues such as constitutional revision, which was favored by a highly vocal segment of the conservatives and bitterly opposed by the progressives. In this context, the progressives perceive the Constitution — despite its fundamentally foreign parentage — as the embodiment of democratic ideals, a view which is not shared by certain leading conservatives, including former Prime Minister Kishi.

These profound differences over fundamental areas of national policy, to the degree that they reflect major fissures in the Japanese body politic, have complicated the traditional Japanese search for consensus and accomodation as it is conducted in the Diet. On a number of notable occasions, the best publicized of which was the 1960 imbroglio over the acceptance of the revised U.S.–Japan Security Pact, these differences have led to a complete breakdown in the Diet's operations. Moreover, it is incorrect to assume that the periodic breakdowns in decorum within the halls of the Diet are the only occasions when this lack of a national consensus has become manifest. It is and has been a constant factor. Only the degree of its intensity has varied.

Second, nearly all of the postwar Cabinets have been the exclusive preserve of the conservatives. Indeed, there was only one brief inter-regnum (1947–8) during which the Socialists shared in the exercise of executive power by participating in two coalition Cabinets. In the first of these (May 1947–March 1948) Katayama Tetsu, a Socialist, served as Prime Minister, a post he relinquished to Ashida Hitoshi, a Democrat (conservative), during the second (March–October 1948). With this limited exception — notable primarily for its brevity, although Socialist purists maintain that their comrades eternally compromised them-selves by participating in these Cabinets and thus have adversely af-fected the party's capacity to gain the full support of the progressive voters — representatives drawn from the ranks of the 'reformists' have not had administrative experience and therefore allegedly lack a sense of responsibility. It might be noted that while valid at the national level, this reproof is not well-founded with regard to the prefectural (provincial) level. Governor Minobe of Tokyo, a Socialist and former Tokyo University of Education professor of Economics, is the best known of several leaders in this category. Nonetheless, in the exercise of executive power at the national level, it is the conservatives who have prevailed.

Third, party leaders demand — and in the overwhelming majority of instances receive — absolute obedience from their followers when there is a formal ballot in the Diet. One notable exception to this generaliz-ation was provided by Shiga Yoshio, a Communist, who decided to defy the wishes of the JCP's leadership by voting for the Partial Nuclear Test Ban Treaty in 1963. For his audacity he was expelled from the party, and he promptly formed the *Nihon no Koe* (Voice of Japan) Communist

45

Party. In this instance, Shiga was responding to Moscow's rather than Peking's signals; the latter were stronger in the JCP at the time. Generally, however, resorting to a specific sanction – e.g. expulsion – is not necessary. Instead, party leaders can rely on the traditional Japanese virtue of loyalty and the extraordinarily strong sense of group identity that is to be found in all walks of Japanese life. Furthermore, all differences of viewpoint will have been thrashed out at an earlier, preparliamentary, stage of the legislative process. For many reasons, then, formal votes in the Diet are nearly always cast along the strictest of party lines.

Since its creation in 1955 the conservative Liberal-Democratic Party has used each of these factors to its own advantage. When it has wanted to do so it has been willing to use the absolute majority that it has consistently won in both chambers of the Diet; it has demanded and received disciplined voting from its members; and it has tried to play the role of consensus-builder – in accord with hallowed tradition – when that has been deemed to be advantageous.

By contrast, the Opposition parties have been relatively impotent over the last quarter century, in large part because they have never come even close to controlling a majority of seats in either chamber. As a consequence, and most particularly when the LDP resorts to tactics of confrontation (which will be elaborated in Chapter 4), the Opposition shout 'Foul!' (what else can they do?) and accuse the LDPers of using their majority in a tyrannical fashion. This indictment has peculiar potency in the context of Japanese society because of the high value that is placed on reaching the broadest conceivable consensus. When this search for consensus fails, as it must, given the ideological disparities that persist, the Diet's decorum is marred by scenes of near violence.

One overriding feature of Japanese political parties renders the foregoing description incomplete, accurate though it may be if attention is accorded only to the formal votes that are cast. Appearances of unity within each of the parties during formal divisions in the Diet are deceptive, for they hide the intense bargaining that has taken place inside the parliamentary parties at earlier stages of the policy-making and legislative processes. Especially in the cases of the LDP and JSP, the facade of unity during Diet votes that each party seeks to project to the public obscures the considerable amount of strife that exists fairly constantly in each. It is the factions (*habatsu*) which are the real actors in intra-party politics in Japan. Their importance, especially in the LDP, cannot be overemphasized. It is the factions which have pro-

Table 7 *Actual party strengths in House of Representatives 1961-73*

Year	LDP	Ind.	Komeitō	DSP	JSP	JCP	Total opposition	Vacant	Total
1961	297	3		16	142	3	161	6	467
1962	295	3		15	142	3	160	9	467
1963	290	3		15	139	3	157	17	467
1964	289	1		23	144	4	171	6	467
1965	283	2		23	145	4	172	10	467
1966	279	3		23	142	4	169	16	467
1967	284	4	25	31	141	5	202		486a
1968	280	4	25	31	139	5	200	2	486
1969	275	2	25	31	137	4	197	12	486
1970	300	3	47	32	90	14	183		486
1971	301	2	47	30	91	14	182	6	491b
1972	296	3	47	29	87	14	177	15	491
1973	284	1c	29	20	118	39	207		491

aSubsequent to reapportionment adding 19 seats to House of Reps.

bSubsequent to reversion of Okinawa Prefecture, adding 5 seats to House of Reps.

cInd. elected with joint backing of JCP–JSP, hence Opposition.

Sources: *Kokkai Binran* [Diet Handbook] (Tokyo: Nihon Seikei Shimbunsha, 1961, 1962, 1963, 1964, 1965, 1966, 1967, 1968, 1969, 1970, 1971, 1972, 1973).

vided the most crucial leavening element in what might otherwise have become an LDP bulldozer and a relatively dull scene.

Factionalism can probably be traced back for many centuries, and is to be found in all segments of Japanese society. Indeed, one way of looking at Japan's modern political history is to view it as consisting of the rise and fall of various *batsu* (the generic root for 'faction'), such as the *zaibatsu* (finance, business and industry), *gumbatsu* (the military), *kambatsu* (civilian bureaucracy), or a particular division of the *gakubatsu* (school or university), not to overlook *keibatsu* (family) *ad infinitum*. Factions have played so central a role in the recent evolution of Japan's political parties that any understanding of the legislative process must begin with a brief elaboration of the reasons for their existence in, and their effect upon, the parties, particularly the LDP and the JSP.

That the LDP is a coalition of factions has become a cliche. Nonetheless it bears repetition if for no other reason than that America's most distinguished ambassador to Japan, Dr Edwin O. Reischauer, at his farewell press conference in Tokyo's Okura Hotel in effect scolded some of the American journalists (and others like myself who were present at the occasion) for being excessively concerned with factionalism in their analyses of Japanese politics. It seems to me that too little attention is accorded to factionalism by either foreign journalists and scholars in writing about or discussing that country's politics. Therefore I would like to invite the reader's attention to the question not of whether, but of why there are factions in the LDP and why they are influential.

First of all, the LDP is like a major river into which various tributaries have flowed. Even in terms of the simplest schematic representation, it is necessary to mention that each of the two major conservative parties that combined to form the LDP, that is, the 'Liberal' and 'Democratic' parties, brought with them their own internal divisions. Hence, the concept of the LDP as two parties brought together under one name is an oversimplification; the Liberal Party had been divided into the Hatoyama and Yoshida wings, and the Democratic Party had gone through a number of different incarnations in the immediate postwar years, each leaving its mark. Given the importance that is accorded to group loyalty in Japan, it is therefore not surprising that there are rivalries among those who trace their initial allegiance to various wings and incarnations. All of the LDPers may quite properly be labeled as conservatives, but the meaning of that label is imprecise and covers a broad spectrum of attitudes. Opposition to the 'progressives' is the principal ingredient that holds them together, as is evidenced by the fact that the LDP came into existence in response to the — temporary — reunification of the Socialist Party.

A second factor, which is becoming considerably less important as the years go by and mortality takes its toll, is the conflict between those conservatives who were temporarily removed from active political life under the Occupation-induced purge of militarists and ultranationalists and those who had emerged as leaders during the years that their brethren were *persona non grata*. Hatoyama Ichirō, the unifier of the conservatives and first president of the LDP, had been declared 'undesirable' by the Occupation on the eve of his election as Prime Minister in the Spring of 1946. At the time, an agreement was ostensibly made between himself and his successor, Yoshida Shigeru, that when Hatoyama would be permitted to return to active political life, Yoshida would restore to him the reins of power. This well-publicized 'secret' agreement was not honored by Prime Minister Yoshida. Earlier supporters of these gentlemen encountered some difficulty, understandably enough, in becoming happy swimmers in the same LDP stream.

A third factor, also exemplified by the Hatoyama—Yoshida split, was and remains the substantial difference in orientation between those who entered political life through participation in local, prefectural or national legislatures as opposed to those who entered from the bureaucracy. In Japanese parlance, this is referred to as the division between *Tōjin* (partymen) and the *Kanryō* (bureaucrats). If Hatoyama epitomized the *Tōjin* by having been re-elected thirteen times to the House of Representatives, Yoshida was the archetype of the exbureaucrat who came to dominate the LDP in the postwar period. Indeed, nearly all of the Prime Ministers have been drawn from the latter ranks: Shidehara Kijurō (Foreign Ministry) 1945—6, Ashida Hitoshi (Foreign Ministry) 1948, Yoshida Shigeru (Foreign Ministry) 1946—7, 1948—54, Kishi Nobusuke (Commerce and Industry Ministry) 1957—60, Ikeda Hayato (Finance Ministry) 1960—4, Satō Eisaku (Transportation Ministry) 1964—72. In this context, the accession of Tanaka Kakuei to the presidency of the LDP and Prime Ministership in the summer of 1972 was a minor revolution. He was not an ex-bureaucrat — and his formal education had ended with elementary school.

Prime Minister Tanaka also reflects some of the ambiguities in the *Tōjin* v. *Kanryō* distinction. He was for many years a loyal retainer in former Prime Minister Satō's faction, and Satō had not only been a bureaucrat, but had been brought into parliamentary politics by Yoshida. In terms of lineage, Tanaka is another graduate of the so-called Yoshida school, which, in the persons of Ikeda and Satō, dominated the pinnacle of the LDP in the 1960s. Despite this kind of imprecision, the distinction between the *Tōjin* and the *Kanryō* is a reality that is felt and that is consequential in intra-LDP maneuvering.

Seiji Shikin (political funds), or to put it less elegantly *o-kane* (money) provides the fourth factor contributing to factionalism in the LDP. While the party is generally conceded to be the wealthiest in Japan (technically, official reports indicate that the JCP —as a party — overtook the LDP in fiscal 1972; but that is misleading since the LDP factions also have their own sources of funds), its wealth is insufficient to support all of its endorsed candidates adequately. By the same token, few candidates can make up out of their own pockets the difference between what the party provides and what is required. Substantial sums are involved. Newspapermen estimated that many LDPers needed one hundred million yen (*ichi-oku yen*), approximately $333,333.00 each, to win and might well lose if they only had seventy million yen (*nana-sen-man yen*) approximately $233,333.00 each in their campaign kitties, which estimates brought a new shorthand phrase '*ittō-nanaraku*' into the highly malleable Japanese language.[1]

This kind of money is not readily available, not even in certain of the increasingly affluent sectors of the Japanese economy. Hence, an aspiring candidate for a Diet seat, after receiving official party funds and contributions from his local supporters, usually finds it necessary to approach one of the faction leaders for about 25% of his campaign budget. Conversely, one of the principal prerequisites for becoming a faction leader (*oyabun*, literally translated 'boss') is the ability to raise political funds. It is to be understood that the sums in Table 8 reflect only those that these major LDP factions have officially reported under the terms of the Political Funds Contribution Law. How accurately they reflect actual income is a matter of considerable controversy. It would probably be fair to conclude that they reflect orders of magnitude, which are useful both for purposes of comparison and as indicators of which factions are in ascendancy and which in decline.

More importantly, even this level of available funding to each faction contributes to an understanding of why factions manage to survive as separate entities. On the basis of officially reported sums for the same periods in the above mentioned report the income of the LDP, as a party, was 5,888 million and 1,898 million for 1971 and 1972 respectively. On that basis, the Ōhira and Tanaka factions each had incomes in excess of one-third of the total for the LDP, the Fukuda faction nearly 28%, the Miki faction 22.6% and so forth for the first six months of 1972. It is no wonder that factionalism continues to thrive within the bosom of the LDP.

The amount of money a faction leader has access to obviously influences the number of LDPers, either as candidates or elected Dietmen, he can help to support, and who are therefore likely to become his followers. This factor becomes particularly salient at LDP conventions. Contests for the coveted post of party president, which automatically brings with it the Prime Ministership so long as the LDP retains its majority in the House of Representatives, are rarely charades. Alliances which are made, coalitions which are built, promises which are kept — and occasionally broken — during the course of these elections for LDP president provide the fifth reason for the persistence of factionalism.

[1]Please see my 'Ittō-Nanaraku: Japan's 1969 General Election', *Asian Survey*, March 1970.

A faction leader's power tends to be a reflection of the number of followers he has in the House of Representatives. Factionalism is less strong in the House of Councillors; and although LDP Members of that House are also voting delegates to the party conventions, their votes are less crucial than those cast by the delegates who are members of the House of Representatives. It is the latter who predominate in the election of the Prime Minister. In this instance the formal allocation of power is mirrored in reality. If the leader has many followers, his ability to bargain with other faction bosses is enhanced, as is his ability to declare his own candidacy for the office of party president. However, the larger the number of his followers, the greater is the drain on his financial resources. Former LDP Vice-President Kawashima Shojirō maintained that the optimum factional size was 25 Representatives. It was his contention that a faction boss could not provide adequate services to his followers if the faction's size exceeded that number. By 'services', he was understood to mean financial support and assistance in securing for his followers Cabinet portfolios, Diet Committee chairmanships, parliamentary vice-ministerships or important party posts. Less than twenty-five Members would result in a loss of influence and bargaining power with the party president or the other faction bosses.[1] Yet, the record indicates that for a leader to have a reasonable chance for success in running to win for the party's presidency — contests for which were held every two years until 1972, but under the new party rules occur only every three years — the minimum number in his faction must be around forty-five Members in the House of Representatives. Thus, Ikeda had fifty-three personal factional followers in the House of Representatives when he became Premier, Satō had forty-nine, and Tanaka forty-three. On the other hand, Kawashima undoubtedly had a point in that excessively large factions tend to develop sub-factions. For example, during the latter years of his Prime-Ministership, Satō's faction had become an unwieldy grouping of about sixty members; the faction really consisted of two separate entities, one pledged to Tanaka, who served Satō as Party Secretary-General for many years, and the other Hori Shigeru, who served Satō as Chief Cabinet Secretary for much of the same period. Hori ultimately linked his fortunes to those of Fukuda Takeo, who in turn ran as the major rival candidate against Tanaka in the July 1972 LDP Convention. Regardless of how questions of money and factional size are dealt

[1]Conversation with the late Kawashima Shojirō, former Vice-President of the LDP in Hakone at a seminar-meeting of his faction to which he had been kind enough to invite me, 8—10 August 1963.

Table 8 Liberal-Democratic Party and major LDP factions' political funds
(*in '000s ¥*)

		Income		1971–1972 Increase or (−) decrease −3,990,000
		Jan.–June 1971 5,880,000	Jan.–June 1972 1,890,000	
	Liberal-Democratic Party			
Ōhira Masayoshi	Shin Sangyō Seisaku Kenkyu-Kai [New Industries Policy Study Association]	112,240	355,700	243,460
	Shin Zaisei Kenkyu-Kai [New Financial Affairs Study Association]	137,710	330,370	192,660
	Total:	249,950	686,070	436,120
Tanaka Kakuei	Etsuzan-Kai [Etsuzan-Association]	151,892	199,240	47,348
	Zaisei Chōsa-Kai [Financial Affairs Research Association]	64,442	143,854	79,412
	Shin Seiki Shinkōkai [New Politico-Economic Progress Association]	23,012	120,987	97,975
	Seiji Keizai Chōsa-Kai [Politico-Economic Research Association]	50,266	107,171	56,905
	Keizai Shakai Kenkyu-Kai [Socio-Economic Research Association]	22,771	96,784	74,013
	Total:	312,383	668,036	355,653
Fukuda Takeo	Jikyoku Keizai Mondai Konwa-Kai [Econ. Circumstances-Problems Conversation Soc.]	137,443	221,836	84,393
	Chiyoda Keizai Mondai Konwa-Kai [Chiyoda Econ. Problems Conversation Soc.]	93,610	199,299	104,689
	Shin Seiji Keizai Kenkyu-Kai [New Politics-Economics Study Association]	55,567	106,914	51,347
	Total:	286,620	527,049	240,429

Miki Takeo	Seisaku Kondan-Kai [Policy Consultation Society]	111,700	350,700	239,000
	Kindaika Kenkyu-Kai [Modernization Study Association]	17,170	78,000	60,830
	Total:	128,870	428,700	299,830
Nakasone Yasuhiro	Kindai Seiji Kenkyu-Kai [Modern Politics Study Association]	67,300	129,767	62,467
	Shin Seiji Chōsa-Kai [New Politics Research Association]	99,860	121,560	21,700
	Sannō Keizai Kenkyu-Kai [Sannō Economics Study Association]	12,000	42,000	30,000
	Total:	179,160	293,327	114,167
Mizuta Mikio	Tatsumi-Kai [Tatsumi-Association]	0	104,550	104,550
	Rissui-Kai [Rissui-Association]	54,900	83,690	28,790
	Total:	54,900	188,240	133,340
Satō Eisaku	Seikei Kenkyu-Kai [Politico-Economic Study Association]	124,066	101,659	−22,407
	Asia Kenkyu [Asia Study]	53,350	36,700	−16,650
	Ikusei-Kai [Political Education Society]	49,300	31,000	−18,300
	Total:	226,716	169,359	−57,357

Source: *Mainichi Shimbun*, 12 January 1973, p. 2. (Courtesy of George O. Totten.)

with, it is clear that contests for the party presidency serve to perpetuate whatever tendencies toward factionalism may already exist.

The unique medium-sized multiple-member district system under which candidates for Japan's House of Representatives are elected provides the sixth factor promoting factionalism. There are 124 districts, each returning three, four or five Members, depending upon the district's population. Voters write the name of one candidate on blank ballots, thus precluding multiple or weighted voting. It is a system which seems to have been peculiarly well-designed to drive campaign managers and their candidates to distraction and despair, and which is exceptionally well-suited to exacerbating intra-party factional strife. Not all parties run more than one candidate per district, of course. For example, until the December 1972 election the JCP had always run only one, but broke with tradition by running two in Kyoto 1st constituency. Both won.

The LDP, however, must run more than one candidate per district since the mathematics of winning a majority of seats in the House of Representatives requires it to do so. The House currently has 491 Members; a bare majority would be 246; but there are only 124 districts. Hence, it is necessary to have two successful LDP candidates per constituency at the very least. Complicating these calculations is the declining strength of LDP support in urban districts. For example, there was one urban district, Aichi 6th (the city of Nagoya) in which no LDP member won in 1972. In effect, this means that the LDP must run more than two candidates in certain rural districts where 'conservative' sentiment remains strong.

Thus the first task of the LDP's leadership is to determine the optimum number of candidates it should endorse. If too many aspirants receive the party's blessing there is the risk that available voting strength will be spread too thin. To endorse too few may embitter candidates who are not anointed and conceivably drive their supporters into the arms of one of the Opposition party's candidates. In the 1972 contest, the LDP endorsed five candidates in Kumamoto 1st district, a five-member constituency. Three were incumbents, each belonging to a different faction (Fukuda, Ōhira and Miki). Of the two newcomers, one had pledged himself to Nakasone, and the other's affiliation was the very small Hayakawa grouping, an offshoot of the Miki faction. What made the whole matter of endorsement delicate was that the LDP had almost consistently won four of the five seats over the last five elections. By spreading itself to endorse the fifth candidate the LDP actually lost a seat, winning only 3 and allowing two Opposition party candidates (the incumbent Komeitoite and a new JSPer) to be elected. Furthermore, one of the LDP incumbents in the Miki faction was supplanted by a newcomer of the Nakasone faction, who had the good fortune of inheriting his deceased father's support organization.

In neighboring Kumamoto's 2nd district, the situation was even more complicated for the LDP. It too was a five-man constituency which had also consistently given four of its seats to the LDP. Endorsement was restricted to four (two Fukuda faction followers, an Ishii supporter, and a Tanaka man). So far so good, but additionally there were six 'Independents' who were running, and all of them were 'conservatives'. What made the situation particularly poignant for Fukuda was not only that two of the incumbents were his followers, one of whom — Sonoda Sunao — was a recent convert who had previously been the leader of his own faction, but also that one of the 'Independents' had been a private secretary or administrative assistant to Fukuda himself. In this instance, the LDP did retain its four seats — despite the district being the home of the infamous *Minamata* disease — but in the process one of the officially endorsed candidates, a follower of Prime Minister Tanaka, was defeated by one of the 'Independents' who surfaced as a Nakasone supporter.[1]

Not all districts provide such difficulties for the LDP. There are some in which the election of their candidates is a foregone conclusion as soon as the formal party endorsements are made, providing — and the proviso is heavy with consequences — the party endorses the right number. One of these is Gumma's 3rd, a district justly famous by having two well-known candidates, Minister of State, and former Foreign Minister, Fukuda Takeo and Minister of International Trade and Industry Nakasone Yasuhiro. It is worth adding that both are also leaders of large factions in the LDP and that the former is a past and still potential LDP presidential candidate, and the latter a likely one for the near future.[2] Table 9 provides an overview of electoral results in this district over the last six elections.

---

[1] Nishihira Shigeki, *Nihon No Senkyō* [Japan's Elections] (Tokyo: Shiseido, 1972), pp. 414–15; *Shugiin Giin Sōsenkyō Rikkohosha* [Candidates for the House of Representatives General Election] (Tokyo: Jiyu-Minshu To [LDP], 23 November 1972), p. 50; *Asahi Shimbun*, 11 December 1972, p. 2.

[2] It is also a district made famous in American analyses of Japanese politics in Nathaniel B. Thayer's *How the Conservatives Rule Japan* (Princeton University Press, 1969), pp. 98–102.

Table 9 House of Representatives election results in Gunma's 3rd district

Candidate	Party	1958	1960	1963	1967	1969	1972
Fukuda Takeo	LDP	88,027	92,099[b]	95,378[b]	100,573[b]	99,466[a]	178,281[b]
Nakasone Yasuhirō	LDP	70,852[a]	76,274[a]	84,504[a]	72,731[a]	106,823[b]	93,879[a]
Kurihara Toshio	JSP	53,237[a]	44,463[a]	44,496[a]	43,348	—	—
Obuchi Mitsuhira	LDP	49,762[a]	Obuchi Keizo (son)	47,350[a]	61,543[a]	50,185[a]	37,258[a]
Mutō Unjirō	JSP	35,457					
Yamaguchi Tsuruo	JSP		39,398[a]	43,774	50,747[a]	59,659[a]	57,909[a]
Shoga Kenji	DSP	—	29,313	—	—	—	—
Niwayama Akira	Komeitō	—	—	—	—	35,942	—
Various Candidates	JCP	5,017	6,330	6,916	9,919	10,764	18,544

Adapted from Nishihira, *Nihon No Senkyō* [Japan's Elections], p. 326 (1958–69) and *Asahi Shimbun* 11 December 1972, p. 2 (1972).

[a]Victor in the four-seat district.
[b]Top victor.

After even a cursory glance at the results of the last three elections one could predict that the voters in Gumma's 3rd would send three LDPers to the House of Representatives, with the fourth seat reserved for a JSPer. Furthermore, given the weakness of the JCP in the district, the results to be obtained on 10 December 1972 were forecast with complete confidence as soon as the LDP and the JSP had made their official endorsements and it was clear that no 'Independent' would be foolish enough to declare his candidacy. What, then, could explain the intensely feverish campaigning that could be observed?[1]

Undoubtedly, the motivations of the campaign workers were varied. One overriding concern that goaded members of the Fukuda or Nakasone camps was the question of which of the two leaders would be returned as *saikō* or 'number one'. Fukuda had attained this coveted position regularly until the 1969 election, during which Nakasone's supporters had put forth a prodigious effort and enabled their leader to emerge triumphant. Fukuda's troops were not inclined to forget that 'debacle' (obviously, merely to win a seat is poor solace), nor were they willing to forgive Nakasone for having supported Mr Tanaka's bid for the LDP presidency at the party convention five months earlier. After all, no citizen of Gumma in Japanese history had ever come as close to becoming Prime Minister as Fukuda had on that occasion — only to have the prize plucked from his grasp with the well-publicized assistance of that 'terrible apostate' Nakasone. Thus on this occasion Fukuda not only came in first, but by a margin of nearly two to one, the largest ever. Mr Nakasone, the third LDPer Obuchi and the JSPer Yamaguchi were all also re-elected as predicted.

As has become amply clear by now, each district has its own characteristics. In nearly all of them, intra-party factional strife tends to be more important than the ostensible battle among the different parties. While these battles between presumed comrades-in-arms can be destructive of party unity (more on that later), they can also, as in Gumma 3, serve to turn out the vote in contests which might otherwise induce voter apathy. Whatever the final balance of pluses and minuses one might wish to draw up, one point is clear: multiple-member constituencies do tend to promote factionalism within the LDP.

[1] Based on a personal tour of Gumma's 3rd district 8 December 1972. I am deeply indebted to Mr Sam Jameson, Tokyo correspondent of the *Los Angeles Times*, who made all the arrangements, and to the campaign managers and workers in Mr Fukuda's and Mr Nakasone's camps who extended every possible courtesy.

The seventh and final factor contributing to factionalism in the LDP is the most difficult to pin down because of its quicksilver properties. What is involved is the whole matter of public policy and the issue of tactics to be employed by the LDP towards the parties of the Opposition. LDPers tend to be highly pragmatic in their approach to politics, or to put it another way, are perfectly willing to permit others the privilege of being ideological or principled. (No implication is intended that ideology and principle are synonymous.) Yet, questions of policy do occasionally contribute to factional strife. Approval of the revised Security Pact with the United States in the spring of 1960 was one such issue, as was the whole question of China policy. On the latter, for example, it was generally conceded that most of the so-called 'Taiwan Lobby' supported Mr Fukuda, whereas most of those favoring the re-establishment of relations with the People's Republic of China were backers of Mr Tanaka in the July 1972 Convention of the LDP. It would be totally misleading to conclude that this division over an issue of policy was the determining factor in trying to explain why Tanaka emerged victorious. At most it was marginal and quite possibly largely fictitious in that even if Fukuda had won he too would have undertaken a rapprochement with the PRC. There might have been a slightly different timetable involved, and there might also have been certain differences in nuance in the Japanese Government's dealings with Taiwan. On elements of basic substance there would have been virtually no difference.

What creates perplexity in attempting to assess the influence of policy as an element in factional strife is its ambiguity. That is to say, one is never certain whether advocacy of an alternative policy contributes to factional strife or, conversely, that the requirements of factionalism demand the espousal of substitute ideas. It has not been uncommon for individuals to change their stands in accordance with whether they were moving into or out of the mainstream coalition in the party. If nothing else — and, on occasion this can be of more than passing consequence — factionalism does assist in the ventilation of alternative approaches to questions of public policy. Whether this process actually promotes factionalism cannot be conclusively answered.

In one respect there does appear to be a fairly constant division between two major groupings of factions in the LDP. On the surface it is a matter of style; at a deeper level it involves fundamental questions of parliamentarism, for at issue is the way in which the LDP as the majority party relates to the parties of the Opposition, especially the JSP and the JCP. Some LDPers are eager to engage in tactics of confrontation, whereas others are far more interested in searching for areas of accommodation or agreement. Those of the former persuasion are generally labeled as belonging to the 'Old Right' (that is more conservative), while the latter have been dubbed the 'New Right' (that is more liberal). These disparate tendencies do exist, but they do not follow factional lines. In other words, a generally 'Old Right' faction such as Fukuda's may well contain some 'New Rightists', whereas such 'New Right' factions as Miki's, Nakasone's, and Ōhira's may also include some staunch conservatives in their ranks. Nonetheless, which style predominates in the coalition controlling a Cabinet profoundly affects the Diet's operations. It, probably more than anything else, determines whether a particular session is going to be relatively stormy or comparatively placid.

While there are too many variables to encourage any absolute gauging of factional influence in the foregoing area, that influence can be measured with considerable accuracy in a related sphere, the making of personnel decisions. The selection of important LDP officials, Cabinet Ministers, Diet Committee chairmen and parliamentary vice-ministers simply cannot be comprehended without considering the role of factions. This theme will recur in various contexts; but for the moment it will be illustrated by using Prime Minister Tanaka's Cabinet established on 22 December 1972 as a case in point.

One noteworthy feature of this Cabinet is the rapidity with which it was formed. The House of Representatives election had been held on 10 December. At its initial plenary session held during the afternoon of the 22nd, the first order of business was the election of the new Speaker and Vice-Speaker. It was a foregone conclusion that the candidates put forth by the LDP would win, and so they did. Nakamura Umekichi (Nakasone faction) was elected Speaker with 300 (of 485) votes and Akita Daisuke (Shiina faction) became Vice-Speaker with 280 votes (of 486).[1] It is noteworthy that both the Speaker and Vice-Speaker belong to factions which are classified as belonging to the *Tōjin* (parliamentarians) wing of the LDP. Those decisions having been made, the next order of business was the formal election of the new Prime Minister. Each of the parties put forth its own candidates,

[1] *Nihon Keizai Shimbun*, 23 December 1972, p. 2.

Table 10   *The Second Tanaka Cabinet, formed 22 December 1972*

Post, Ministry	Name	Age	No of times elected	District	Faction
Prime Minister	TANAKA Kakuei	54	11	Niigata 3	Tanaka
Justice	TANAKA Isaji	66	12	Kyoto 1	Ishii
Foreign Affairs	ŌHIRA Masayoshi	62	9	Kagawa 2	Ōhira
Finance	AICHI Kiichi	65	7 + 1*	Miyagi 1	Tanaka
Education	OKUNO Seisuke	59	4	Nara	none
Welfare	SAITO Kunikichi	63	6	Fukushima 3	Ōhira
Agric. and Forestry	SAKURAUCHI Yoshio	60	9 + 1*	Shimane	Nakasone
Internal Trade and Industry	NAKASONE Yasuhirō	54	11	Gumma 3	Nakasone
Transportation	SHINTANI Torasaburō	70	5*	Nara	Ishii (Tanaka)
Posts and Telecomm.	KUNO Chūji	62	10	Aichi 2	Tanaka
Labor	KATŌ Tsunetarō	67	9 + 1*	Kagawa 2	Miki
Construction	KANEMARU Shin	58	6	Yamanashi	Tanaka
Autonomy (Home)	ESAKI Masumi	57	11	Aichi 3	Mizuta
Deputy Prime Min. Dr. Gen'l Envir. Agency	MIKI Takeo	65	14	Tokushima	Miki
Chief Cabinet Sec.	NIKAIDO Susumu	63	9	Kagoshima 3	Tanaka

Table 10 continued

Education	Occupation	Selected prior important posts
Central Tech. Sch.	Business; construction	Min. of Post & Telecomm., Finance, Int. Trade & Ind.; LDP Policy Bd. Chr., Sec. Gen'l.
Ritsumeikan U.	Lawyer, local assembly	Min. of Justice, Autonomy (Home)
Tokyo U. of Commerce (Hitotsubashi)	Finance M. bureaucrat	Min. of Foreign Affairs, Int. Trade & Ind.; Chief Cabinet Sec.; LDP Policy Bd. Chr.
Tokyo U. —Law	Finance M. bureaucrat	Min. of Foreign Affairs, Justice, Autonomy (Home); Dir. Gen'l. EPA; Chief Cab. Sec.
Tokyo U. —Law	Home M. bureaucrat	Admin. Vice-Min. Autonomy (Home); Director LDP Gen'l. Affairs Bureau
Tokyo U. —Law	Labor M. bureaucrat	Admin. Vice-Min. Labor; Deputy Chief Cab. Sec.; LDP Deputy Sec. Gen'l.
Keio U. —Econ.	Corp. exec.	Min. of Transp.; Min. of State, Science Bd. Deputy Chr.; LDP Deputy Sec. Gen'l.
Tokyo U. —Law	Writer; parliamentarian	Min. of Transp.; Min. of State, Science & Tech. Agency, Defense Agency
Tokyo U. —Law	Post. and Telecomm. Min. bureaucrat	Min. of Post & Telecommunications
Tokai Middle School	Business; Construction	LDP Policy Bd. Dep. Chr.; Chr. HR Committees: Constr., Cabinet, Educ, House Mgt.
Mukden For. Laws	Steamship co. exec.	Chr. HR Committees: Posts & Telecomm., Construction
Tokyo Agric. Coll.	Construc. co. exec.	LDP Diet Policy Comm. Chr.
Nihon U. —Econ.	Corp. exec.	Min. of State: Defense Agency (twice); LDP Diet Policy Comm. Chr.
Meiji U.—Law	Parliamentarian	Min. of Comm., Transp., Int'l Trade & Ind., Foreign Affairs; Min. of States Econ. Pl. Agency, Science & Tech. Agency; LDP Sec. Gen'l, Policy Bd. Chr.
U. of S. Calif.	Foreign & Navy Ministry bureaucrat	LDP Deputy Sec. Gen'l (twice); Chr. HR Comm.: Construc., Commerce & Ind.

Table 10 continued

Post, Ministry	Name	Age	No of times elected	District	Faction
Dir. Gen'l. P.M. Office and Okinawa Dev. Agency	TSUBOKAWA Shinzo	63	9	Fukui	Fukuda
Dir. Gen'l Admin. Mgt. Agency	FUKUDA Takeo	67	9	Gumma 3	Fukuda
Dir. Gen'l. Defense Agency	MASUHARA Keikichi	69	4*	Ehime	Fukuda
Dir. Gen'l. Econ. Planning Agency	KOSAKA Zentarō	60	12	Nagano 1	Ōhira
Dir. Gen'l Science Tech. Agency; Chr., AEC	MAEDA Kazuo	63	3*	Wakayama	Tanaka
Major Liberal-Democratic party officers					
President	TANAKA Kakuei	54	11	Niigata 3	Tanaka
Vice-Pres.	SHIINA Etsusaburō	74	7	Iwate 2	Shiina
Chr., Policy Bd.	KURAISHI Tadao	72	11	Nagano 1	Fukuda
Chr., Exec. Council	SUZUKI Zenko	61	11	Iwate 1	Ōhira
Sec. Gen'l.	HASHIMOTO Tomisaburō	71	10	Ibaraki 1	Tanaka
House of Representatives presiding officers					
Speaker	NAKAMURA Umekichi	71	12	Tokyo 5	Nakasone
Vice-Speaker	AKITA Daisuke	66	10	Tokushima	Shiina

Note: * = HC. Au others HR.

Table 10 continued

Education	Occupation	Selected prior important posts
Fukui Mil. School	City Mayor	Min. of Construc.; Chr. HR Comm.; Commerce and Ind., House Mgt.
Tokyo U. —Law	Finance Min. bureaucrat	Min. of Agric. & For., Finance, Foreign Affairs; LDP Policy Bd. Chr., Sec. Gen'l.
Tokyo U. —Law	Home Min. bureaucrat	Min. of State: Dir. Gen'l. Defense Agency (twice); Governor, Kagawa Pref.
Tokyo U. of Commerce (Hitotsubashi)	Corp. exec.	Min. of Labor, Foreign Affairs; LDP Policy Bd. Deputy Chief.
Tokyo U.	Post & Telecomm. Min. bureaucrat	LDP Deputy Sec. Gen'l; Chr. HC Comm.: Transportation

Major Liberal-Democratic party officers

Education	Occupation	Selected prior important posts
Central Tech. Sch.	Business; construction	Min. of Post & Telecomm.; Finance, Int. Trade & Ind.; LDP Policy Bd. Chr., Sec. Gen'l.
Tokyo U. —Law	Commerce and Ind. Min. bureaucrat	Min. of Int. Trade and Ind., Foreign Affairs, Chief Cabinet Sec.; Chr. LDP Exec. Council.
Hosei U. —Law London U.	Industrialist	Min. of Labor (twice), Agric. & For. (3 times); Chr. HR. Comm.: Agric. and For. (4 times)
Agric. & For. Res. Inst.	Agric. & For. Org. Official	Min. of Welfare, Chief Cabinet Sec.; LDP Deputy Sec. Gen'l.
Waseda U.-Polit. Econ.	Newspaperman	Min. of Transp., Construc.; LDP Exec. Council Chr.

House of Representatives presiding officers

Education	Occupation	Selected prior important posts
Hosei U. —Law	Lawyer	Min. of Justice, Construc., Educ.; LDP Policy Bd. Chr., Exec. Council Chr.
Tokyo U. —Econ.	Parliamentarian	LDP Foreign Affairs Research Council Dep. Chr.; HR Comm. Chr.; Educ., Soc. Lab., Foreign

Sources: *Sankei Shimbun* 23 December 1972, p. 1; *Nihon Keizai Shimbun* 23 December 1972, p. 2; *Shugiin Yōran* (HR Directory), 1972; *Kokkai Binran* (Diet Handbook), July 1972.

and the resulting vote, conducted within minutes of each other in both chambers, was:

	House of Representatives	House of Councillors
Tanaka Kakuei (LDP)	280	128
Narita Tomomi (JSP)	116	60
Nosaka Sanzo (JCP)	40	10
Takeiri Yoshikatsu (Komeitō)	29	23
Kasuga Ikkō (DSP)	20	12

Balloting in both chambers, for which not all members were present (which accounts for the totals not adding up to 491 and 252 respectively) was concluded shortly before three o'clock in the afternoon.[1] By 8.30 that same evening the entire Cabinet was ready to depart for the Imperial Palace for the formal attestation ceremony. Within two hours, everyone had returned to the Prime Minister's official residence for the first formal Cabinet meeting.

Several other points – aside from the unusual rapidity of the Cabinet's formation, reflective of the prior negotiations that had been conducted and the extraordinary degree to which Mr Tanaka was in charge – require brief elaboration. First, and I believe foremost, Prime Minister Tanaka followed a pattern that has by now become traditional in creating cabinets: he constructed one which mirrored the current balance of factional forces in the LDP. Six portfolios went to important members of his own faction including himself, three to Ōhira's, three to Fukuda's, two each to Nakasone's, Miki's, and Ishii's, one to Mizuta's, and one (the thorny post of Education Minister) to Mr Okuno, who is among the very few Representatives having no factional affiliation.

Second, the specific portfolios accorded to each faction once again reflected the comparative standing of each faction *vis-à-vis* the Prime Minister. Tanaka's faction not only had the Prime-Ministership, but also the crucial Finance Ministry portfolio as well as the post of LDP Secretary-General; Ōhira's the Foreign Ministry, the Economic Planning Agency and the chairmanship of the LDP's Executive Council; Nakasone's, the two significant International Trade and Industry (MITI) and Agriculture and Forestry Ministries plus the Speakership of the House of Representatives; Miki's the high-status Deputy Prime-Ministership; while Fukuda's was accorded three 'Agencies', which although headed by a Minister of State, are relatively low on the pecking order, with Defense being the only conceivable exception (and even

[1] *Loc. cit.*

64

its standing is higher in the eyes of foreigners than of the Japanese). These relatively low-ranking posts were partially offset by the selection of Mr Kuraishi (Fukuda faction) to the important chairmanship of the LDP's *Seichō-Kai*, Policy Affairs Research Council.

In Mr Fukuda's case there were problems for all concerned. He had been Tanaka's principal opponent for the LDP presidency five months earlier. No one had forgotten that contest. Moreover, Fukuda had powerful enemies inside the party, not the least of whom were Nakasone (viz. Gumma 3) and important members of Mr Miki's faction, as well as those of Mr Ōhira and Mr Shiina. Should Prime Minister Tanaka invite his arch-rival to join and thus guarantee himself a burr in the saddle; and, conversely, should Fukuda allow himself to accept an invitation if it came, thereby limiting his capacity to act as a critic? As noted, he was asked to join, and he did so. Out of the welter of motives, two related ones are conceded to have been crucial. Gains made by the Opposition parties, especially the JCP and the JSP, and the relative decline of the LDP provided one powerful goad. The other was the resultant need for unity among the Liberal-Democrats; and what kind of Party unity could there be if the leader of the largest faction (Fukuda) were not in the Cabinet? In the end, the circumstances required that Prime Minister Tanaka bring all major faction leaders into the Cabinet.

Finally, two ancillary factors provided proof of the weight of tradition in Premier Tanaka's personnel decisions at the apex of Japanese politics. As before, eight of the twenty Cabinet Ministers were Tokyo (Imperial) University graduates. Second, nine of these gentlemen had begun their careers as bureaucrats. Tanaka himself might be a plebeian, but as yet there were no fundamental changes in the continuity of prerequisites providing access to the top. It was, by and large, a Cabinet of tested and experienced veterans. Factionalism had triumphed again.

Factionalism is also a fact of life for the Socialists, who are still the largest party in the 'progressive' house in Japanese politics. In certain respects the JSP is even more badly split than the LDP. In the early 1950s there were two Socialist parties, the 'Right' and the 'Left'. Since January 1960, there has existed an unrepaired fission between the major JSP and the increasingly minor DSP. Many JSPers would reject the notion that the DSP is still in fact a 'socialist' party. Viewed from the perspective of the Second Internationale, the DSP is akin to the British Labour Party or the SPD in West Germany. Its leadership is moderate in its policies and more fully dedicated to parliamentarism

Table 11 *LDP Factions 1962–73*

	1962^c HR^a	HC^b	1963^c HR	HC	1964 HR	HC	1965 HR	HC	1966 HR	HC
⌐Ikeda Yoshida	53		50		48	11	Maeo 47	15	47	15
└Satō	53		49		45	49	44	52	44	52
Kaya	5		3							
	Fukuda	25		17		20	1		20	
Kishi 42 ——→	42		4		5		18		18	
	Kawashima	25		18		18		18	Nanjo
Fujiyama	40		24		21	12	18	11	18	11
Ishii	23		14		15	19	14	10	14	10
Ōno	32		29		29	12	16	9	3	9
							→Murakami	11		
							→Funada	12		
Matsumura-Miki	33		32		37	12	37	10	36	10
Ishida	6		4							
									Mori-Sonoda	
⌐Kōno Hatoyama	34		31		47	18	46	14	←44	14
									Nakasone	
└Ishibashi	4		4							
Unaffiliated	2		2		8	8	16	16	15	15

^aHR = House of Representatives; ^bHC = House of Councillors.
^cMany double entries in HR; factions not yet formalized in HC.

Sources:
Watanabe Tsuneo, *Habatsu* [Factions] (Tokyo: Kobundo, 1964), pp. 181–91.
Kokkai Binran [Diet Handbook] (Tokyo: Nihon Seikei Shimbunsha, 1962, 1963, 1965, 1966, 1967, 1968, 1969, 1970, 1971, 1972).
Yomiuri (Shimbun, mimeo., n.d., but 13 December 1972) and private inquiry 1 February 1973.

than any other party in Japanese politics. An influential segment of Japan's academic and intellectual communities finds in the DSP a respectable haven, while at the same time allowing it to be critical of the LDP. Yet, as a party, it is no more than the smallest of the Opposition groupings.

Of the three major factions in the JSP itself, the Eda and Katsumata factions are comparatively moderate in their ideology, while the Sasaki faction perceives itself as militantly Marxist, or rather, Marxist in a

Parties, factions and the Diet

Table 11 continued

1967 HR HC	1968 HR HC	1969 HR HC	1970 HR HC	1971 HR HC	1972 HR HC	1973 HR
42 11	43 18	43 18	44 19 Ōhira	43 18	43 19	44 Ōhira
57 52	54 46	45 46	59 46	60 ⌐44 ⊢Tanaka ⌐Hori—	42 39	47 Tanaka
23	28 8	28 8 ⌐	→38 18	39 20 "new"	65 28	53 Fukuda
17	17	17 │	20 Shiina	18 4	17 4	18 Shiina
	6 —	6—				
17 9	7 10	7 10	6 2	6	3	
14 10	13 9	13 9	12 9	13	13 5	9 (Ishii)
10 3			Mizuta	4	→16 2	14 Mizuta
10 3	10 3	10 3	10 3	10 2⅃		
15 6	13 5	13 5	14 5	12 4	10 4	9 Funada
4	4	4	3 kawasaki	3	3	
35 10	37 10	37 10	42 9	42 12	⌐39 11	39 Miki
				└→Hayakawa 3		
			6	6┘		
4 5	11	11	14	14—		
15		12		7	7	
	25	25	36 16	35	33	39 Nakasone
24						
11 4	8 18	8 18	5 12	5 25	14 17	9 Unaffiliated

Maoist way. Indeed, if there is a significant difference which distinguishes factionalism in the JSP from that in the LDP, it is that the Socialists take their ideological commitments considerably more seriously. Moderates may — and do — accuse the hard-liners of being excessively concerned with 'ideological purity', especially with regard to insisting that the JSP be a 'class party', which the moderates believe to be counter-productive to prospects for enlarging the potentially available popular support for the JSP. In turn, the militants accuse their comrades of not being 'sincere', an attribute of profound significance, in their commitment to socialism, and worse of being ready to sell out to the conservatives who rule Japan. One of the reasons for the emotion-laden quality of these debates is the unpleasant memory from the 1930s of many of the party elders diluting their principles by becoming staunch nationalists and thereby supporters of Japan's militarist policies.

Another difference between the LDP and the JSP is that if the LDP's conventions tend to be models of propriety on the surface (infighting

67

Table 12 *Socialist factions in the Diet (HR = H. of Representatives; HC = H. of Councillors)*

	1961 HR	HC[a]	1963 HR	HC[a]	1965 HR	HC	1966 HR	HC	1967 HR	HC
Nishio-DSP	16		15		23	7	23	7		
Kawakami	27		25		25	7	22	7	Kōno Mitsu 18	7
Eda					10	24	19	24	26	23
Wada	35		35		34	12	37	12	Katsumata 29	12
Unaffiliated-neutral			3		18	6	15	10	10	6
Suzuki-Sasaki	45		9⌐ 14		41	24	36	24	14	26
Nōmin (Agric.) Doshikai (friends)			5	1	4	1	3		3	1
Kuroda	4⌐									
Leftists	8→									
Heiwa (Peace) Dōshikai (friends)	18		→15		11		10			

[a]Factions not yet organized in House of Councillors.
Based on: *Kokkai Binran*, 1961, 1963, 1965, 1966, 1968, 1970, 1971, 1972, 1973.

takes place behind the scenes) and thus rather lackluster affairs, the JSP's conventions are raucous and filled with sound and fury. Its 33rd Convention, held 20–1 April 1970, almost could not take place because the Han-sen Seinen Iinkai (Anti-war Youth Committee), an important JSP support organization made up of students and young blue-collar workers, was almost successful in barricading the doors leading into the Kudan public hall. They made the attempt because they feared that the delegates would adopt a 'moderate' platform and elect a 'moderate' central committee, 'moderate' from the perspective of the Han-sen Seinen Iinkai, of course. Not until the arrival of the *kido-tai* (riot police), whose activities the Socialists tend to deplore, and some physically robust mine-workers, who joined in shoving the obstruction-ists from the massive doors, could the delegates enter and begin their

Table 12 continued

1968 HR	HC	1969 HR	HC	1970 HR	HC	1971 HR	HC	1972 HR	HC	1973 HR	HC	
31	10			32	10	30	13	29	13	20	13	
16	2		2	14						4		New Eda
23	7	23	7	15		30		29		29		Eda
29	7	29	7	22		21		20		25		Katsumata
					33		33		31		29	
14	29	14	29	15	10	21	18	21	20	27	19	Neutral
		Yamamoto		4								
44	19	44	19	16	20	16	14	16	14	38	14	Sasaki
			3		3		2		2		2	
										3		Shakai Shugi Kyokai [Socialism Assoc.]
8				4		1		1		2		Anpō-Funsai Dōshikai [Crush Security Pact Friends]

deliberations.[1] The balance of the convention was held behind closed doors.

In other respects, JSP factionalism has many of the same attributes as that in the LDP. The JSP also is a party that was created out of a diversity of prewar parties. It too has its quota of purgees and non-purgees. 'Parliamentarians' vie for positions of leadership with trade union bureaucrats. In turn, different unions tend to support different factions with campaign contributions, though this is hard to prove with exactitude. Contests for positions of leadership in the party at its conventions also contribute their share to the longevity of factional-

[1]For details, please see *Nihon Shakaitō Dai Sanju-san-kai Rinji Zenkoku Taikai Sokkiroku* [Proceedings of the thirty-third JSP National Convention] (Tokyo: JSP, n.d., but 1970). It should be added that I was among the observers of the proceedings and was given special dispensation to depart and return by way of subterranean passages leading to back doors which were not barricaded.

ism in the JSP. Finally, the JSP too is faced with the need to run more than one candidate in the multiple-member constituencies. It is only with respect to the intensity with which matters of ideology are felt and debated that the JSP differs from the LDP. It is generally conceded that the LDP — by being more successful — has managed to cope with factionalism better than the JSP. It is a conclusion with which I agree.

Japan's Communist Party (JCP) has not been immune from factional strife, despite its disciplined organizational structure. Ideological disputes plagued the party even during the prewar period when it was illegal. Unlike other Japanese parties the JCP suffered by an excess of foreign control which was often heavy-handed and all too often was more reflective of the Kremlin's politics than a response to Japanese circumstances. After a short period of relative freedom in the initial years of the Occupation era during which the party flourished and succeeded in creating a 'lovable' image, it suffered, in 1950, two nearly fatal blows. It was badly shaken by the Cominform's stern criticism, and while responding to that by adopting a more militant posture fell foul of the Occupation authorities, who proceeded to declare most of the party's leadership ineligible to hold public office. Many of the party's younger leaders fled into exile in Peking, and upon their return to their homeland established themselves as a 'China Lobby' in the late 1950s and early 1960s. By then, the party was faced with trying to cope with the Sino—Soviet dispute, a reality that the leadership had tried to avoid. In effect, three groupings emerged: the 'China Lobby', which was also sometimes referred to as the 'young officers', the older Kremlin-oriented group, and — for want of a better descriptive term — the 'nationalists'.[1]

Since 1966, however, factionalism in the JCP has been kept to a minimum under the astute leadership of Praesidium Chairman Miyamoto Kenji, who gives every indication of having succeeded in emphasizing the 'Japan' in the party's name. As noted, the party's fortunes are in the ascendant under Miyamoto's *jishu-dokuritsu rosen* (autonomously-independent line). Some remnants of the 'China Lobby' still exist, as—to a lesser extent — do the older Kremlin crowd. Power is in the hands of Miyamoto and his younger followers such as Fuwa Tetsuzo, Ueda Kōichirō, and Matsumoto Zemmei. Under their leadership, the JCP has regained respectability — almost too much

---

[1] Please see my 'Yoyogi and Its Rivals' in Robert A. Scalapino, ed., *The Communist Revolution in Asia*, 2nd. ed. (Englewood Cliffs, N.J.: Prentice-Hall, 1969), pp. 212—33.

for some of the younger student radicals in the hard-left anti-JCP wing of the Zengakuren (National Student Federation) who talk as if the JCP has become one more segment of Japan's establishment. With these minor caveats, the party for the moment is relatively free of factionalism. To the degree that it exists at all it is under the strictest kind of control, as is evidenced by its ability to successfully run two candidates in one district. In Kyoto's first district Taniguchi Zentarō and Umeda Masaru came in first and third respectively in a five-man district, a feat which required iron discipline in the distribution of votes between them. In all of the other districts the party continued to run only one candidate, so that the tendency towards factionalism that sets in under the pressures of multiple candidacies in the same constituency was not present.

Little factional strife is as yet to be noted in the Komeitō (Clean Government Party). Its extremely rapid growth in the 1960s (see Table 4) very possibly assisted in preventing its members from engaging in internal infighting. Everyone was far too busy 'making it', so to speak. Furthermore, as in the case of the JCP, the Komeitō has only run one candidate per district. It has even gone one step further by importing potential Komeitō supporters (that is members of Sōka Gakkai) from neighboring constituencies in order to ensure — insofar as possible — that one of its candidates would be assured of having enough votes to win. This was possible under the election law so long as the voters transferred their place of residence and officially registered three months prior to the election. One of the reasons for the decline of the Komeitō in the 1972 election was allegedly that it had not expected the election to take place until the spring of 1973, and thus had not had time to move its supporters around in advance of 10 December.

Until that election for the House of Representatives the Komeitō had never really confronted the whole range of emotions associated with a decline in political strength. It is too early to assess whether doing so will bring forth the bitter internecine struggles that, for example, have wrought havoc inside the JSP when it has had to sort out the reasons for a 'defeat'. It is of course possible that the doctrines of Nichiren Shoshu will provide sufficient unity to prevent factionalism from appearing in the Komeitō. However, it would be surprising if that should prove to be the case in the long run.

There can be little doubt that factionalism exists as a fact of life — probably the basic fact of life — in Japanese politics. Disagreements arise, however, over the worth of its continued existence in the conduct

71

of that country's politics. Many members of the academic and intellectual communities criticize factionalism because, for them, the *batsu*
are an atavistic remnant of Japan's feudal past. Furthermore, they
contend that Japan's political party system cannot become modern or
truly rational so long as these factions — which by their very nature
tend to emphasize the role of personality in politics and the bonds of
loyalty between a leader and his followers (the *oyabun-kobun* relationship) — interfere with the goal of doing what is best for Japan. Policies
cannot be developed and decisions cannot be made on the basis of some
abstract notion of rationality, it is averred, so long as factionalism
interferes by introducing the presumably non-rational personal
element into the political process.

I disagree, and for several reasons. The structure of the Japanese
political party system is the basic element. There is every likelihood
that the Liberal-Democratic Party will continue to be the majority —
and hence governing — party for the foreseeable future, given the
relative weakness and disunity of the Opposition parties, i.e. the JSP,
DSP, Komeitō and JCP. For the time being, they have extremely limited
prospects of becoming a majority if for no other reason than that they
are divided.

Second, if the foregoing is a reasonably accurate forecast of trends of
Japanese politics, then the LDP — if it were an absolutely united party —
might become authoritarian or its President (in his capacity as
Prime Minister) might become dictatorial. While this latter contingency
is unlikely, given the submergence of the individual in the group which
in itself has provided a barrier against dictatorship in Japan, oligar-
chical authoritarianism is a danger against which factionalism has
been, and has every prospect of continuing to be, an important protective shield.

Third, factions allow different segments of the Japanese public to
have influence, and thereby allow alternative ideas, policies and legislative proposals to have supporters and opponents inside the party which
governs Japan. It is inside the majority party, in the pre-parliamentary
negotiations, that the fundamental decisions are made, and it is therefore vital that alternative proposals be ventilated at that stage of the
policy-making process. One can of course argue that even with the
existence of factions in the LDP the spectrum of views which have their
spokesmen in the highest policy-making councils of the Japanese
Government is insufficiently broad. That may be true in ideal terms.
Relatively speaking, however, so long as factions exist there will cer-

tainly be a broader spectrum of views which must be taken into account than if they were abolished.

In conclusion therefore, factions and factionalism contribute their share to making Japanese politics more open and competitive. In the context of Japan's political party system, factionalism is not only advantageous, but also eminently rational. Furthermore, only by coming to terms with the intra-mural disputes that take place within the political parties themselves, can one come to grips with the realities of Japanese politics.

CHAPTER THREE

Innai[1] *Seido:* **the parliamentary system**

An impressive ceremony reminiscent of Japan's imperial past marks the beginning of each Diet session. It is held in the main chamber of the House of Councillors which, under the Meiji Constitution, had been the home of the House of Peers. It is the only House of Parliament into which the Emperor has ever entered, to the best of everyone's recollection. Architecturally, there is only one major distinction between the plenary chambers of the two Houses. In the House of Councillors the imperial throne is located in an alcove directly behind the presiding officer's chair, and there is a royal box in the center of the visitors' gallery. These features are absent in the House of Representatives' plenary chamber.

Attendance at the *kaikai-shiki* (opening ceremony) by the Members is not mandatory although most generally appear out of a sense of duty, an important ingredient in Japanese behavior especially on ceremonial occasions. A hush settles over the audience as word spreads that His Imperial Majesty is about to enter the chamber to read the Message from the Throne.[2] He enters and mounts the few steps leading to the imperial alcove. The presiding officer's rostrum has been removed for the ceremony in order that His Majesty can see and be seen by the assemblage. The Emperor, Hirohito, who ascended the throne in 1926 and has had the longest reign in Japan's modern history, proceeds to read his Rescript in a high, quavering voice, giving every appearance of being more than just a little ill at ease.

I have observed the official convocation of a Diet session on three separate occasions. Each time, the Emperor's message has impressed me as being the very model of vague generalizations. Ambiguous

---

[1] *'Innai'* literally translates as 'inside the House(s)', but it is only used with reference to the Diet.

[2] The Emperor, with the advice and approval of the Cabinet, shall perform the following acts in matters of state on behalf of the people ... Convocation of the Diet...', The 1947 Constitution of Japan, Chapter I, Article 7, *The National Diet of Japan* (Tokyo: Diet print, 1960), p. 5. The Communists boycotted the opening ceremony of the 1973 Session on the ground that the Emperor's presence was unconstitutional.

allusions are made to the problems confronting Japan and the Members are urgently requested to devote themselves to their solution, and to do so as expeditiously as possible. It is all reminiscent of a somewhat aging teacher pleading with a potentially unruly classroom of students to behave themselves and press on with their assignments. As ritual it compares favorably with the prayer preceding an American President's State of the Union Message to the United States Congress, more than with the Message itself.

Prior to the Emperor's ceremonial appearance, hosts of bureaucrats are hard at work in planning for the oncoming Diet session. Officials in the *Sōri Kantei* (the Prime Minister's Official Residence) and in the *Sōri-Fu* (Prime Minister's Office), as well as in the headquarters of the Liberal-Democratic Party are busily formulating policies, programs and strategy. One of their priority items is helping the Prime Minister to prepare his 'State of the Nation' message, which reviews past accomplishments and presents his analysis of current issues and suggests ways in which they are to be met. In a separate message and more reality-oriented, his Finance Minister will submit the Government's Budget.

Bureaucrats in the various Ministries and Agencies also have been assisting their Ministers in formulating policies and programs that might be submitted to the Diet. Normally, at an early session the Foreign Minister will read a message setting forth Japan's foreign policy goals for the coming year; other Ministers may also be called upon, depending upon what issues are of special salience at the time. If trade and balance of payments problems loom large, for example, the Minister of International Trade and Industry might be asked to prepare a special message setting forth the Government's views. It is to be emphasized that in each instance the ministerial bureaucrats play an indispensable (possibly controlling) role in the preparation of these communications.

On occasion, the Prime Minister and his Cabinet might convene an extraordinary Diet Session for the resolution of one specific, particularly pressing item of national business. This was the case in the fall of 1965, for example, when the major item on the Diet's agenda was the passage of the treaty reestablishing normal diplomatic relations between Japan and the Republic of (South) Korea. If such is the case, then all Cabinet messages of the opening meetings of that session will be primarily concerned with the pertinent proposed legislation, concerning which the Constitution commands that the Diet's approval be obtained.[1]

[1] The 1947 Constitution of Japan, Chapter IV, Articles 60 and 61, *ibid.*, p. 15.

The content and character of these various messages vary depending on whether they signal the start of an 'ordinary' (*tsujo*), 'extraordinary' (*rinji*), or 'special' (*tokubetsu*) session. Ordinary sessions are convened in December and last for one hundred and fifty days, unless extended by vote of the Members. Only one extension is allowed. An extraordinary session may be convoked by the Cabinet or by a vote of one fourth of the Members of either House. A special session must take place within thirty days after a general election for the House of Representatives. A vote in both chambers, held concurrently, determines the length of an extraordinary or special session. Both extraordinary and special sessions can be extended twice.[1]

The ritual of the Emperor's speech, the Ministerial messages, and opposition questions and presentation of their goals, might be compared with the key signature on a piece of music which later develops atonally. It is functional only in the sense that it allows the Cabinet, in which executive power is vested,[2] to point out its goals and the Opposition to announce contrapuntally how it proposes to thwart them. However, form prevails over substance; what is actually possible of achievement is determined elsewhere, principally within the LDP, the majority party.

Before turning to the roles of the political parties in the Diet, it is necessary to provide a brief sketch of the internal organizational structure of the two Houses and to give some indication of the services that are available to the Members in accomplishing their mandate. Formally, it is the presiding officer who is in charge. 'The President of each House shall maintain order in the House, adjust its business, supervise its administration and represent the House.'[3] There is some confusion in the English terminology regarding the proper translation of *Gicho* (literally, chairman of chamber). In the official version of the Diet Law, *Gicho* is translated as 'President'. The 'Rules of the House of Representatives', however, refer to him as 'Speaker', whereas those of the House of Councillors designate the presiding officer as 'President'. In any case, it is he who presides, formally speaking.

Presiding officers and their deputies (i.e. Vice-Speaker and Vice-

---

[1] The 1947 Constitution of Japan, Chapter IV, articles 52–4, *ibid.*, pp. 12–13. The Diet Law, Chapter I, Articles 2 and 3; Chapter II, Articles 10–13, *ibid.*, p. 26 and pp. 27–8.

[2] 'Executive power shall be vested in the Cabinet.' The 1947 Constitution of Japan, Chapter V, Article 65, *ibid.*, p. 16.

[3] The Diet Law, Chapter III, Article 19, *ibid.*, p. 29.

President) generally come from the ranks of the majority party. For a variety of reasons, immediately prior to their installation in these posts, some of these leaders designate themselves as 'Independent' (*mushozoku*, literally 'without party affiliation') in the official Diet Directory.[1] This label, however, does not signify the kind of non-partisanship and impartiality that is generally associated with the Speaker of the British House of Commons, but has a different origin altogether.

House of Councillors' President Kōno Kenzō and Vice-President Mori Yasoichi who were elected in the summer of 1972 are cases in point. Both designate themselves as 'Independent'. Both were originally members of the Ryokufu-kai (Green Breeze Society), a group that was a section of the LDP in all but its official name. Moreover, President Kōno is the younger brother of the late Kōno Ichirō, who was one of the early major LDP faction leaders, later headed by Minister of International Trade and Industry Minister Nakasone, and who in the autumn of 1964 had bitterly and unsuccessfully contested Satō Eisaku for the LDP presidency and the concomitant Prime-Ministership. For the greater part of Prime Minister Satō's tenure, one of his closest allies in the LDP had been Shigemune Yūzo, President of the House of Councillors and leader of the Satō faction (by far the largest in the LDP) in that chamber.[2] In fact, the ties between Satō and Shigemune were said to be so close that the Prime Minister's views were assured of prevailing in the House of Councillors. Ultimately it was these ties — which some Councillors apparently believed to be excessively close — which led to the minor revolt in the House of Councillors after the 1971 election. Kōno and Mori sought and received support from disgruntled LDPers as well as from the ranks of the Opposition parties.

In one respect their election signalled the declining influence of Satō, at least among LDPers in the House of Councillors. In another respect it could be interpreted as an assertion of independence by that chamber *vis-à-vis* the Prime Minister, his Cabinet and the more powerful House of Representatives. If so, it was true only briefly. One year later Mr Nakasone played an influential role in making Tanaka President of the LDP. Kōno Kenzō, the new President of the House of Councillors, had been a member of his brother Kōno Ichirō's faction before labelling himself an 'Independent'. That faction was then under the leader-

---

[1] *Shugiin Yōran* [House of Representatives Directory] and *Sangiin Yōran* [House of Councillors Directory] (Tokyo: Okura-Shō Insatsu-kyoku [Finance Ministry Printing Office], published after each election.)

[2] About 45 out of a total of 136, or about one-third.

ship of Nakasone, who was himself an important member of the Tanaka Cabinet and the mainstream coalition supporting the Prime Minister in the LDP. Hence, it is believed to be far more likely that Kōno's becoming President of the House of Councillors anticipated more a shift away from Satō among LDP factions in the House of Councillors than the onset of an era of autonomy for the presiding officer of that chamber. In its essentials it was an intra-LDP factional dispute which could have longer-range implications when and if the LDP ever loses its majority among the Councillors.

In both Houses the Diet Law commands that the presiding officers be elected by a majority of the Members of that Chamber.[1] This formal requirement is not violated in the election process itself. Prior thereto, each party will have made its decision as to whom to support. In most instances — Kōno and Mori's election was a noteworthy exception — the candidates put forth by the LDP will win. Furthermore, as was noted in the last chapter, the LDP leadership makes the selection for Speaker and Vice-Speaker in the House of Representatives in conjunction with the formation of a new Cabinet. Hence, it is within the context of Cabinet-making, which — as noted — requires the proper balancing of factional alignments inside the LDP, that the real nominations are made.

House of Representatives Speaker Nakamura Umekichi and Vice-Speaker Akita Daisuke were elected on 22 December 1972, at the opening session after the general election of 10 December just prior to the formation of the 2nd Tanaka Cabinet. Nakamura is a member of the Nakasone faction and Akita of that led by former Foreign Minister and current LDP Vice-President Shiina Etsusaburō, a faction inherited from the late LDP Vice-President Kawashima Shōjirō, who had been close to Prime Minister Tanaka while he was LDP Secretary-General.[2] Both factions had been important elements in the coalition supporting Tanaka for the LDP presidency the previous July. Both factions belonged to the partymen's wing (*Tōjin-ha*) of the party, notable in that the posts of Speaker and Vice-Speaker are generally reserved for non-bureaucrats. Additionally, both Speaker Nakamura and Vice-Speaker Akita had had lengthy careers in the House and had held a number of

---

[1]'In case the post of the President or the Vice-President, or of both, has become vacant, an election shall be held without delay to fill the vacancies.' The Diet Law, Chapter III, Article 23, *The National Diet of Japan*, p. 29.

[2]For details of the Kawashima-Tanaka alliance, please see my 'Ittō-Nanaraku', *Asian Survey*, March 1970, pp. 189—94.

important party posts and Government offices. Nakamura had just been re-elected to his twelfth term in the House of Representatives; he had been Minister of Justice, of Construction, of Education, chairman of the LDP Policy Board (*Seichō-kai*) and Executive Council (*Sōmu-kai*), as well as chairman of the party's Diet Policy Committee (*Kokkai Taisaku Iinkai*), the most crucial link between the party and the Diet's internal machinery. Akita had just begun his tenth term. He had been Minister of the Autonomy (Home) Ministry, Deputy Secretary General of the LDP, Deputy Chairman of the party's Diet Policy Committee and Deputy Chairman of the LDP's Foreign Affairs Research Council.[1]

Both Nakamura and Akita exemplify the qualities that the LDP leadership emphasizes in making its nominations for Speaker and Vice-Speaker: lengthy tenure and wide-ranging experience. Others who have filled these posts, the most important in running the affairs of the House, have had basically similar backgrounds since the middle of the 1960s. From 1958 through 1964 Speaker Kiyose Ichirō governed the House as an 'Independent', although he had been a member of the Democratic Party. Formerly a lawyer and a judge, Kiyose tried to emulate the Speaker of the British House of Commons in running the affairs of the House of Representatives, at least so he told me.[2] Unfortunately, his tenure included the most serious parliamentary crisis that the Diet has had to face in the postwar era, the imbroglio over the Security Pact renewal in the spring of 1960. Kiyose's role in that lamentable episode is controversial, at least in terms of the model on which he sought to pattern his leadership. Circumstances simply did not permit him to play the role of quasi-judicial arbiter between the principal antagonists of the day, the Liberal-Democrats and the Socialists. It would have been superhuman to do so in the face of the Socialist efforts, which were partially successful, to lock him in his office and to use sit-down tactics in the halls of the Diet building to prevent him from opening a plenary session.[3]

Another feature of Speaker Kiyose's term of office for its first four years was that his Vice-Speaker was a Socialist Representative. Kubota

---

[1] Biographical data based on *Shugiin Yōran*, 1970 edition, p. 149 and p. 11 respectively.

[2] Interview with House of Representatives Speaker Kiyose Ichirō, in his chambers 31 May 1963.

[3] For further details of Speaker Kiyose's role and the tribulations he suffered, please see George R. Packard III, *Protest in Tokyo: The Security Treaty Crisis of 1960* (Princeton University Press, 1966), *passim*, but especially pp. 237–9, 240–1, 275–6.

Tsurumatsu had been elected to the Vice-Speakership in 1958 with the expectation that the LDP and the JSP would agree on the fundamental rules of parliamentarism, a presupposition that was sundered by all parties concerned in the agony of May-June 1960. That searing experience came perilously close to tearing apart the very fabric of the Diet itself, and all that has transpired since then can to some considerable degree be seen as an effort to repair that damage.[1] As for the Speaker and Vice-Speaker, it had effectively ended the cooperative experiment, in which Representatives drawn from different parties shared leadership responsibilities. With the 1962 Diet session, the tradition of electing both from 'conservative' ranks was established, Hara Kenzaburō, a trusted LDPer of then LDP Vice-President Ōno Bamboku's faction, becoming Kiyose's deputy. Moreover, beginning with the 1964 session and the election of Funada Naka as Speaker, this office too has been held by a regular LDPer.

Funada, who was Speaker 1964–5 and again from 1970 through 1972, was another senior parliamentarian. He was in his eleventh term at his first election to the post and had previously served as Minister of State, Director-General of the Defense Agency and Chairman of the LDP's Policy Board. He had also inherited the leadership of the larger portion of Ōno Bamboku's faction, which had split after the death of that colorful figure in 1964. Funada had the misfortune of being Speaker during the fall of 1965 when Prime Minister Satō and the entire LDP succeeded in pushing through the first major item of serious controversy since the spring of 1960, namely the treaty reestablishing normal diplomatic relations between Japan and the Republic of Korea. As a price for continuing to participate in the parliamentary process, the Socialists demanded that Funada resign from his post; they accused him of exercising the duties of his office in a dictatorial fashion.[2] After some delicate and necessarily private negotiations had been conducted, Prime Minister Satō acceded to the JSP's ultimatum; in the end Funada did have to be sacrificed for the sake of institutional survival. As noted, it was a temporary penance.

---

[1] For another interpretation of those events, please see Robert A. Scalapino and Masumi Junnosuke, *Parties and Politics in Contemporary Japan* (Berkeley and Los Angeles: University of California Press, 1962), pp. 125–53.

[2] For details, please see my 'Nikkan Kokkai: The Japan–Korea Treaty Diet' in Lucian W. Pye, ed., *Cases in Comparative Politics: Asia* (Boston: Little, Brown, 1970), pp. 19–57.

For Prime Minister Satō it was a minor price to pay the Socialists. After all, with Speaker Funada's help the treaty had been approved.

After a brief term during which Yamaguchi Kikuichirō held the title of *Gichō* in the immediate aftermath of the Korea Treaty fracas, Ishii Mitsujirō was Speaker for most of the latter half of the 1960s. Ishii too was a senior parliamentarian, being in his ninth term when elected to the Speakership. Earlier, he had been an official in Japan's colonial administration in Taiwan as well as an executive in the *Asahi* newspaper empire. He had also been Minister of Commerce, of Transportation, of International Trade and Industry, and of Justice, as well as having been Deputy Prime Minister, Secretary-General of the Liberal Party and Chairman of the LDP's Executive Council. Most important of all, he was the leader of a faction and had contested for the presidency of the LDP in 1960 against Ikeda Hayato (who won) and former Foreign Minister Fujiyama Aiichirō. His willingness to accept the Speakership was something of a triumph for Prime Minister Satō, who prided himself on his handling of personnel matters. Not only did Ishii bring a wealth of experience and, consequently, prestige to the leadership of the House of Representatives, but also he was thereby effectively neutralized from again running for the LDP presidency. There is the as yet uncontested assumption that once one has accepted the Speakership one has removed oneself from the ranks of those seeking the party presidency. His final major achievement was to supervise the passage of the immensely controversial Emergency University Administration Law, which empowered the Minister of Education to intervene in the governance of Japan's strife-ridden institutions of higher education. At the time, the opposition parties once again tried to man the barricades; because they perceived the proposed legislation as granting the government excessive powers, a view that was shared by most editorial writers. The law was adopted, but for his role in its passage, Speaker Ishii was forced to resign, though remaining as an elder statesman in the House until his retirement just prior to the 1972 general election.[1]

Not only did the LDP tighten its grip on the Speakership by the end of the 1960s; but the posts of Speaker and Vice-Speaker became progressively more and more enmeshed in LDP factional politics, possibly one consequence of the increasingly formalized structure of intra-LDP factional politics. Each of the nominations supports this generalization

---

[1]Biographical details based on *Shugiin Yōran* 1967, p. 1.

to some degree, but the selection of Arafune Seijūrō as Vice-Speaker illustrates it best.

During 1966, relations between Prime Minister Satō and his party vice-president Kawashima Shōjirō had cooled perceptively. So delicate (to use a Japanese expression which is favored when inter-personal communication has become strained) had they become that Mr Kawashima refused to become vice-president of the LDP at its convention in December. In turn, Satō did not ask anyone else to assume that party office. To do so might have created an irreparable breach, and the LDP Constitution did not command that there be a party vice-president at all times.[1]

Arafune, a member of the Kawashima faction, had himself been a major figure in the deterioration of relations between Satō and Kawashima. His career as Minister of Transportation in the July 1966 Satō Cabinet had been brief and stormy. He had seen to it that an express train would make an additional stop at a station that had virtually nothing to commend it except that it was in the midst of his constituency (Saitama 3rd). He had also been unusually blatant in requesting that private builders who had contracts with the Transportation Ministry funded projects become contributors to his organization of campaign supporters. What irked Kawashima was not that Satō required Arafune's resignation after these malfeasances had been publicized, but that another Cabinet Minister, Defense Agency Director-General Kambayashiyama Eikichi, who had the good fortune to be a Satō faction loyalist, was nor forced to resign despite having indulged in equally, if not more, grotesque behavior. That was the real affront.

Three years later, and after Kawashima had once again become LDP vice-president, Satō completed the healing of the breach that had existed between them by agreeing to Arafune's becoming the party's nominee for Vice-Speaker of the House of Representatives. To be sure, Arafune did have some qualifications, having served as chairman of the Budget Committee on three separate occasions. However, it is unlikely that he would have become Vice-Speaker had it not been for Kawashima's influence and Satō's need to mollify his senior party colleague.

What does all of this signify? First, the presiding officers of each chamber of the Diet increasingly have become pawns in working out intra-LDP factional politics. This comments obviously applies more

[1] I first learned of this possibility while attending a *yo-mawari* (newspaper-men's term for their late evening rounds) at the home of Mr Kawashima 3 November 1966.

fully to the Speaker and Vice-Speaker in the House of Representatives than to their counterparts in the House of Councillors. Second, the impact of this process has been to make the leadership of each House increasingly subservient to the dictates of the LDP's leadership, especially to that of the party president and the coalition of factional leaders supporting him in his capacity as Prime Minister of the Cabinet. Third, this has contributed to the heightened power of the executive in controlling the affairs of the Diet, and conversely has decreased the capacity of the presiding officers to carve out areas of autonomy for themselves, although it is questionable whether they ever had much independence. Fourth, these posts have become the almost exclusive province of LDP factions which tend to be dominated by party-men (*Tōjin*), as opposed to ex-bureaucrats. All of the four Speakers, Funada (Ōno-Funada faction), Yamaguchi (Kōno), Ishii (Ishii) and Nakamura (Nakasone) as well as six of the last seven Vice-Speakers, Hara Kenzaburō (Funada), Tanaka Isaji (Ishii), Sonoda Sunao (Kōno), Arafune (Kawashima), Hasegawa Shirō (Kawashima) and Akita (Kawashima-Shiina) are themselves long-term parliamentarians and are affiliated with party-men's factions. Only Kodaira Hisao of the recent Vice-Speakers belongs to a 'bureaucratic' grouping, that of Foreign Minister Ōhira. Kodaira is himself not a former bureaucrat, but an automobile corporation executive. His affiliation with Mr Ōhira is provided by university ties; they are both graduates of the Tokyo College of Commerce, now Hitotsubashi University. Hence, he too is not a real exception.

Formally, the presiding officers of each chamber are its leaders. They are accorded a plenitude of powers by the Diet Law and the 'Rules' of their respective Houses. Some of these powers are crucial. It is they, for example, who control the 'order of the day', that is the agenda.[1] In the final analysis, however, it is the Prime Minister who controls the presiding officers of the Diet.

A standing committee of each House assists the Speaker and President in exercising their formal powers. The Committee on House Management (*Giun Un'ei Iinkai*, usually referred to as *Giun*) is the focal point for regulating the internal affairs of each chamber.[2] Despite their

---

[1] Rules of the House of Representatives, Chapter VIII, Section 2, Article 108; and Rules of the House of Councillors, Chapter VIII, Section 2, Article 87. *The National Diet of Japan*, p. 91 and p. 133 respectively. (Hereafter, these will be cited as 'HR Rules' and 'HC Rules'.)

[2] HR Rules, Chapter VII, Section 5, Article 92, Paragraph 15; and HC Rules, Chapter VII, Section 4, Article 74, Paragraph 15; p. 85 and pp. 129–30 respectively.

importance these committees are not independent of external control, although one of its past chairmen told me that he hoped to elevate it to a position comparable to that enjoyed by the Rules Committee in the U.S. House of Representatives.[1] Instead, the *Giun* is the central link between the representatives of all political parties in the Diet and the institutionalized structure regulating the flow of business in each House. Linkage is provided by a simple device. It has become customary for each parliamentary party to select the deputy chairman of its Diet Strategy Committee (*Kokkai Taisaku Iinkai*, normally abbreviated *Kokutai*) to serve as one of the *Giun's* directors, who in turn control the affairs of each chamber's Committee on House Management.[2]

Chairmen of the *Giun* rank just below the presiding officers of each House. Generally, only senior parliamentarians — eighth or ninth termers — are honored by being elected to this committee's chairmanship. Kaifu Toshiki, who was elected chairman of this committee in the House of Representatives in December 1972 is a notable exception. First elected in 1960 when he was only twenty-nine years old, his advance inside the Diet has been meteoric. He is a dyed-in-the wool parliamentarian belonging to the faction led by Deputy Prime Minister Miki, himself in his thirty-fifth year in the House of Representatives. Kaifu's appointment to this prestigious post at an early age clearly marks him as one of the most important of the new generation of Representatives. It also reflects concern on the part of the LDP's leadership for individuals in the Diet who can effectively deal with opposition party representatives, especially in the context of the gains posted by the JCP in the 1972 election. Kaifu is among that handful of LDPers who has won the hard-earned respect not only of his seniors in the LDP, but among Representatives of all the parties.[3]

Important as the House Management Committees are in the inner workings of each House, their decisions are not independent of external

[1] Interview with House of Representatives *Giun* Chairman Sasaki Hideyo in his chambers 31 May 1963.

[2] Interview with DSP Secretary-General Sasaki Ryōsaku who had previously served as chairman of his party's Diet Strategy Committee. In his Diet office 18 June 1970.

[3] Mr Kaifu has granted me a number of interviews since the summer of 1963, the last being over lunch in the Tokyo Hilton on 15 June 1972. The viability of the House of Representatives as a parliamentary institution would be assured if its membership included a majority as able as he. (Biographical data are based on *Shugiin Yōran*, 1970, p. 56.)

controls. Committee directors come from the ranks of each party's Diet Strategy Committee. In turn, each of the parliamentary party committee rosters is selected in conjunction with the whole process of personnel adjustment that takes place when the LDP puts together a new Cabinet or the JSP reorganizes its party leadership. Inevitably, factional balancing is involved. Hence, the visible actors who are on the House Management Committee not only reflect the dictates of their respective parties, but also those of their factional leaders. These strings which control their behavior complicate the process of searching for areas of agreement or compromise between the tactics that each party's Diet Strategy Committee has determined upon. The members of the House Management Committees thus are not free in their negotiations but are agents of hostile — on occasion warring — camps.

The system by means of which the goals of all of the parliamentary parties can be adjusted and meshed can work very smoothly. Let us assume that the item before the House Management Committee is the following day's plenary session agenda. Let us further assume that the only question before the committee is how much time is to be alloted for the formal presentation of a standing committee's report concerning a proposed bill that is non-controversial. Prior to the *Giun's* formal discussion of this issue, each party's Diet Strategy Committee will — on the basis of prior information — have arrived at its decision concerning the bill which is to be brought before the plenary session. The members of the House Management Committee, having received their instructions from their respective parties' leadership, will have little difficulty in arriving at the schedule for the plenary session, all parties having conceded that the proposed bill is non-controversial. The plenary session becomes nothing more than a staged formality, but one — and this is crucial — in which all parties have had a share in planning. Estimates vary in accordance with the criteria used in defining what is 'controversial', but all Dietmen that I have interviewed agreed that the bulk of the legislative business is conducted in this fashion.

It is also a system that occasionally becomes badly clogged. If a party's Diet Strategy Committee has decided that the proposed legislation is controversial, it will so instruct its representatives on the Committee on House Management (*Giun*). Discussions inside the *Giun* may become interminable; and agreement on, for example, the agenda for the plenary session may elude the committee altogether. If the *Giun's* members cannot arrive at a consensus, the matter will have to be referred to a meeting among the Secretary-Generals of all the parliamentary parties. By then, the machinery for handling the day-to-day affairs of the House will, in all probability, have broken down. Should the Secretary-Generals succeed in arriving at an understanding they will instruct each of their parties' Diet Strategy Committees which will hand on their decisions to the Committee on House Management for its ratification. Everyone involved will heave a sigh of relief, and the Diet's machinery will again be functioning.

Occasionally – one example being the approval of the treaty re-establishing diplomatic relations between Japan and Korea – even the Secretary-Generals cannot find a formula that satisfies all of the parties. In that event, the Speaker may intervene and attempt to arrange a meeting among the supreme party leaders, the President of the LDP (who is Prime Minister), and the Chairmen of all the opposition parties; but some of the latter may not wish to resolve the impasse, which objective can most easily be achieved by not accepting the Speaker's invitation. Furthermore, the Prime Minister might not wish to commit himself to participating in such a meeting without some reasonable assurance that an agreement will eventuate from it. A total standstill will ensue.

How long it lasts varies. It really depends on whether the LDP leadership decides whether to employ its control over the majority or whether it is willing to engage in behind-the-scenes negotiations with representatives of the opposition parties – and, of course, how willing the latter are to participate in such negotiations. *Hanashiai* ('consultations') have the advantage of being peaceful, but may be interminable and thus interfere with the LDP's overall timetable for a Diet session. This alternative also entails risks for the Opposition party leaders as these negotiations rarely take place inside the Diet itself, but instead in a *machiai* (literally a 'house of assignation', but with, in this case, strictly political implications). Being known to have participated in such a meeting – especially if a resolution of the impasse in the Diet appears to be a by-product of some unknown negotiations – inevitably opens oneself to dark allegations.

Another option that is available to the majority party is for its leadership to have the Speaker (or, President in the House of Councillors) convene a plenary session of the House on his own authority, i.e. by bypassing the entire elaborate system that exists to ensure the participation of all parties in running the internal affairs of the Diet. Presiding officers are empowered to exercise this prerogative by a crucial provision of the Diet Law:

The President of each House shall fix the order of the Day and notify it to the House in advance.

In case the President deems it urgent, he may call a plenary sitting by notifying merely the date and time of such sitting to the Members of the House.[1]

If read and interpreted literally, a presiding officer has the authority to be a dictator in his chamber. His exercise of this power entails risks. Members of Opposition parties may attempt to barricade him in his office, or boycott the session altogether, or allow the session to begin and participate in a variety of delaying tactics that make it impossible to make any progress in the deliberation of the legislative matter which has brought about the impasse in the first place. These impediments, which are political rather than legal, constitute a powerful set of constraints on the excessive use of this grant of power to a presiding officer.

Nonetheless, there are occasions when all alternatives to its exercise have been exhausted. Indeed, the kind of confrontation that ensues has its advantages. It allows all of the participants to prove that they have kept faith with their particular public — the LDP by ramming the legislation through, the Opposition parties by putting their own bodies on the barricades. Better that than to be accused of engaging in under-the-table deals! Well and good, so long as all participants understand the rules of this kind of parliamentary game, if that is what it actually is.

In summary, an elaborate machinery exists whereby all parties which have more than twenty representatives in the House can participate in managing its affairs. Its functioning rests on the willingness of all concerned to use it. Periodically, this will is not present. When it is not, the majority party — through the presiding officer — manages the affairs of the House according to its own dictates. Doing so is possible, but has deleterious consequences. In other words, it is not flaws in the Diet's legal procedures which prohibit adjustment and compromise among different viewpoints. Instead, it is that some legislative issues are so politically volatile that the search for compromise is an exercise in futility.

[1] The Diet Law, Chapter vi, Article 55, *The National Diet* p. 37. This provision is buttressed by the following words. 'When the Speaker deems it necessary, or upon [a] Member's motion, he may alter the order in the agenda, or add new items to it after consulting the House without debate.' HR Rules, Chapter viii, Section 2, Article 112, *ibid.*, p. 89; and 'When the President recognizes it necessary, or when such a motion is made by a Member of Members, the President may alter the order of the agenda by referring it to the House to decide upon it without debate.' HC Rules, Chapter viii, Section 2, Article 88, *ibid.*, p. 134. The full significance of these 'rules' will become apparent in the next chapter.

Diet committees[1]

The Diet's current committee structure is a postwar innovation. Previously the Imperial Diet had functioned with the assistance of three categories of committees: (1) Committee of the Whole House; (2) Standing Committees for the Budget, for Audit, for Discipline, and for Appeals; and (3) Special (in effect 'Select') Committees to examine legislative bills. Gradually, as the legislative work-load increased, the role of the select committees in scrutinizing proposed legislation acquired some degree of significance. An effort was made in the mid-1930s to formalize this nascent development by establishing permanent subject-matter committees, but this effort was aborted.[2] Procedurally, the plenary session (*honkaigi*) remained the core of activity in the Imperial Diet as well as the locus for the deliberation of all legislation.

As part of the 'democratization' of the Japanese political system — and most particularly that of the Diet — the Occupation authorities, which controlled Japan's destiny in the years immediately after the Second World War, altered the internal structure of its national parliament. It is hardly surprising that the new Diet Law incorporates certain features of American Congressional practice and procedure, given the dominant influence of the United States in the ostensibly Allied enterprise.

The most significant part of the Diet Law, the chapter dealing with standing committees, parallels in several important respects the United States Legislative Reorganization Act of 1946. The system of standing committees more than anything else differentiates the House of Representatives from the British House of Commons and gives the Diet a strong resemblance to the United States Congress. Whether the Diet becomes 'the highest organ of state power and the sole law-making body', or continues to pursue its historic role as a

---

[1]Much of this section is based on a paper I prepared for a British Social Science Research Council conference on 'Committees in National Legislatures' held in London, September 1971. The British SSRC's support for research is gratefully acknowledged.

[2]*Waga Kuni ni okeru Iinkai Seido no Jittai ni tsuite* [Concerning the actual administration of our country's committee system], pp. 97—8. This handwritten report was prepared for me by staff members of the House of Representatives Secretariat's Committee Bureau (*Iin-bu*) in the spring of 1970. I am extremely grateful to this Bureau's Deputy-chief Ogyū Kei'ichi and his associates Hirano Sadao and Horiguchi Ichirō for their unstinting assistance in helping me to gain some understanding of the Diet's current committee system.

mere organ of discussion, will depend, in the last analysis, upon the degree to which the standing committees use the powers conferred upon them and the skill with which they employ the legislative aids and devices provided in the Diet Law.[1]

Brave and prophetic words, which have overtones of a possibly misplaced self-assurance. For, grafting a system of standing committees, most of which have specific subjects of legislation as their realm, onto a basically parliamentary system has provided Japanese legislators with one of their most difficult structural problems. American Congressional practice — at least in theory — rests on the Constitutional doctrine of the separation of powers. Its theoretical foundation is the sharing of political power on a basis of equality and distinction. By contrast, as should be more than evident by now, Japanese parliamentary theory and practice rests on a different premise, namely, that there is a fusion of power between the executive and the legislature, with the Cabinet in effect acting as the Diet's executive committee. By adapting it to their own requirements Japanese parliamentarians have succeeded in making the system operational, despite its obvious anachronistic features.

There are sixteen Standing Committees in each House which 'shall examine the bills (including draft resolutions), petitions, and other matters which may come under their respective spheres of work'.[2] These are the Cabinet, Local Administration, Judicial Affairs, Foreign Affairs, Finance, Education, Social and Labor Affairs, Agriculture Forestry and Fisheries, Commerce and Industry, Transportation, Communications, Construction, Budget, Audit, House Management, and Discipline Committees.[3] Twelve of them, as their names indicate, have jurisdictions that parallel one or more of the national government's Ministries. For example, that on Foreign Affairs has the sphere of the Foreign Ministry, that on Social and Labor Affairs those of the Welfare and Labor Ministries, etc.

The Committee on the Cabinet has a broader jurisdiction. It concerns itself not only with the work of the Cabinet and the Prime Minister's Office, but also with those agencies which have not as yet attained the status of a Ministry. Among the most noteworthy of the latter is the

[1]*PRJ*, Vol. I, p. 164.
[2]The Diet Law, Chapter V, Article 41, *The National Diet*, pp. 34–5.
[3]HR Rules, Chapter VII, Section 5, Article 92 and HC Rules, Chapter VII, Section 4, Article 74 spell out the jurisdictions of each committee, *ibid.*, pp. 82–5 and 125–30 respectively.

Self-Defense Agency, but there are others such as the Administrative Management Agency as well. It is these twelve committees which constitute the core of the system.

Two of the other four standing committees concern themselves with internal Diet matters, and two with fiscal affairs. The Committee on House Management (*Giun*) is, as noted, a kind of Rules Committee. Its province is the Diet Law, the 'Rules' of the House, matters referred to it by the presiding officer, the impeachment of judges, and the affairs of the Diet Library.[1] Its work is significant in running the affairs of each House even if it cannot function effectively at all times. By contrast, its companion, the Committee on Discipline — which is to consider disciplinary action against Members of the House and the qualification of Members — is rarely heard from.

A similar distinction is to be made between the remaining two committees. That on the Audit — which has as its jurisdiction the work of the Board of Audit — has been noteworthy primarily for its ineffectiveness. It is the *Yosan Iinkai* (Budget Committee) which has real clout. Its importance does not lie in supervising the formulation of the Government's Budget, which is supposed to be its sphere of jurisdiction.[2] That is accomplished by the bureaucrats in the Ministry of Finance in conjunction with the leadership of the governing Liberal-Democratic Party. The Budget Committee's significance rests instead on its having become the forum for the questioning of Cabinet Ministers on all matters of policy regardless of whether these queries are in any way related to an item in the Budget. Subjects which are raised range all the way from Japan's defense posture to why the moving sidewalks at the Osaka International Exposition were dangerous to life and limb.

Sessions of the Budget Committee, whether in the House of Representatives or House of Councillors, have become one of the few forums in which Members can air real or imagined grievances with all aspects of government policy in a relatively open fashion. That is to say, arrangements for what is to transpire at the open committee meeting have been programmed by the Committee on House Management and the directors of the Budget Committee itself. Once these steps have been taken, attendance by Cabinet Ministers and other Government officials whose presence has been called for is mandatory. A session

---

[1] HR Rules, Chapter VII, Section 5, Article 92, Paragraph 15; and HC Rules Chapter VII, Section 4, Article 74, Paragraph 15, *ibid.*, p. 85 and pp. 129–30 respectively.

[2] *Loc. cit.*, Paragraph 13, p. 85 and p. 129 respectively.

of the *Yosan Iinkai* is the closest the Diet has come to creating a replica of the famous 'Question Time' in the British House of Commons. There is, of course, nothing comparable in the American Congress.

Open Budget Committee meetings, some of which are televised, serve an extremely useful function in informing the public regarding specific aspects of the government's policies. More often than not, the questions posed by Members, especially those belonging to Opposition parties, are more informative than the answers provided by attending Cabinet Ministers and their bureaucratic assistants. They can be as evasive in their responses — possibly even more so because of the marvelous indirectness and ambiguity that are such treasured attributes of the Japanese language — as other political leaders whose native tongue tends to be more precise.

Unfortunately it is virtually impossible to measure the effectiveness of these 'Interpellations', as they are called. Their entertainment value can be considerable, but their influence on official Government policy is virtually impossible to assess. What can be asserted with some confidence is that these Budget Committee meetings provide an opportunity for the interlocutors and their respondents to score points with the attentive portion of the public. These may later be utilized during electoral campaigns, even if their immediate impact is probably negligible. Furthermore, the possibility of questions being raised in the Diet exerts some influence on the handling of controversial affairs of state. This must be so, otherwise Cabinet Ministers would not complain about the time they and their assistants are required to devote to these committee sessions.[1]

Establishment of special committees in both Houses is also provided for in the Diet Law and the 'Rules' of each chamber.[2] They may be created at any time, but most are established at the beginning of each session of the Diet. Ostensibly their role is to examine matters which do not fall within the purview of the standing committees. This rationalization is not entirely sufficient to justify their existence. Work that has been handled by the 'Special Committee on Okinawa and the Northern Islands' could readily have been handled by the existing Committee on Foreign Affairs. Likewise, that of the 'Special Committee

---

[1]Personal interviews with current or past Cabinet Ministers whose anonymity must be respected.

[2]The Diet Law, Chapter v, Article 45; HR Rules, Chapter vii, Section 6, Article 100; and HC Rules, Chapter vii, Section 5, Article 78, *The National Diet*, p. 34, pp. 86–7, and p. 131 respectively.

on Traffic Safety' really comes under the jurisdiction of the standing Committee on Transportation. In these and other instances, the purpose was either to give the Government or the Opposition parties an opportunity to focus the Diet's attention on a particularly pressing problem, or to remove an issue from the influence of vested interests to which the existing standing committee might be excessively responsive, or possibly both.

Many of the special committees virtually acquire the permanence of standing committees, except that they are not specifically named in the Diet Law. Hence, they must be formally re-created at the beginning of each session. As always, there are exceptions. Both Houses established special committees to consider the treaty re-establishing diplomatic relations with the Republic of Korea, attached agreements concerning fishing rights that both Japan and Korea sought to protect, and related domestic legislation which sought to codify the legal status of Koreans resident in Japan. Various reasons were given to justify the 'one package – special committee' approach even though several standing committees could have deliberated on its components – the treaty itself by the Foreign Affairs Committee, the Fishing Agreement by the Agriculture Forestry and Fisheries Committee, the domestic legislation by the Judiciary Committee and so forth. Most observers generally agree that the governing LDP elected to use the special committee device in that instance in order to control the entire legislative process, and most particularly, the timetable of deliberations in the Diet. If such was its purpose, the maneuver almost backfired.

Opposition party leaders, principally those within the Socialist Party, conveniently found it advantageous to experience great difficulties in selecting Members from their ranks who were willing to serve on the special committees which the LDP wanted to establish in each House. This stratagem of the Socialists was strictly in consonance with their overall strategy of delay and procrastination, and one element of their effort to prove that they were doing all they could to prevent the treaty's approval. By comparison, the process of selecting the full complement of members who are to serve on standing committees is usually completed with dispatch at the beginning of each session. In the end, the special committees on the Japan–Korea Treaty each had a little over one week to actually deliberate on the single most controversial political issue of 1965. Their work done, these special committees died, unlamented.[1]

---

[1] *Nikkan Kokkai.*

In each House, formal appointment powers of Members' committee assignments are in the hands of the Speaker and President of the respective chambers. Their discretion is circumscribed by legal requirements and political constraints. The Diet Law commands that each party must receive seats on each committee proportionate to its overall numerical strength in the House.[1] This same proviso has been made to apply to the 'directors' (*riji*) of a committee, although this is rooted more firmly in custom than in the formal 'Rules' of the Houses.[2] *Riji* participate, with the chairman, in running the committee. Their meetings are not public, which allows them to negotiate compromises of conflicting viewpoints more freely than the open meetings of the full committee.

Politically, it is the leadership of each parliamentary party that controls the making of committee assignments. More often than not, the key actor in the process is a party's Secretary-General. He too is constrained, particularly in the cases of the LDP and JSP, by the requirements of maintaining intraparty factional harmony. Assisting in the sorting process is each party's Diet Strategy Committee (*Kokutai*) which becomes the official channel of communication to the House Management Committee. It in turn becomes a committee on committees in formalizing committee assignments which are finally ratified by the presiding officer. The entire process helps a party's leaders in assuring that they will be able to control what transpires in a committee. They can shift Members from one committee to another at will. This is especially crucial in the LDP, of course, for so long as it retains a working majority in each House it can, through its majorities on each committee and of its directorate, regulate the entire legislative process.

All Members, unless they are serving as Cabinet Ministers or Parliamentary Vice-Ministers who are equivalent to Parliamentary Under-Secretaries, must have at least one committee assignment. Attitudes toward service on a committee vary from party to party, but generally

---

[1]The Diet Law, Chapter v, Article 46, *The National Diet*, p. 35.

[2]HR Rules, Chapter vii, Section 1, Article 38; HC Rules, Chapter vii, Section 1, Article 31, *ibid.*, p. 73 and p. 118 respectively. *Riji* are supposed to be co-opted from among the committee's entire membership. In reality, the *Giun* initially determines the ratio of party representation on each committee's *Riji*. Each party thereupon draws up its list of recommended candidates who are submitted by the chairman of the committee to its membership for formal approval. Based on interview with Mr Ogyū and his associates in the Committee Bureau on 18 May 1970 and their *'Iinkai Seido'*, pp. 21–3.

it is considered a duty or obligation (*gimu*) rather than an opportunity. Most LDPers view committee deliberations as a waste of time. They know that their party's position will prevail by the weight of their numbers if nothing else, and that this position has been hammered out beforehand. Opposition party representatives, while agreeing with this assessment, also added their own sense of frustration which originates in their inability to alter an LDP-sponsored legislative bill no matter what they do in committee. A Komeitō Member put it most forcefully and succinctly, 'Committees are a kind of *kazarimono* (ornament)'.[1]

By contrast to mere membership on a committee, the chairmanship — especially of important committees such as Budget and House Management — does carry prestige and is therefore sought after. Legally, standing committee chairmen are to be elected in each house from the ranks of each committee's membership. In practice, it is the presiding officers of each House who make the appointments; however, they only ratify decisions that have been arrived at in intra-LDP and inter-parliamentary party consultations.

The process works slightly differently in each House. As is apparent from Tables 13 and 14, the House of Councillors allocates committee chairmen in proportion to the numerical strength of the parliamentary groups in that chamber. Two factors vitiate the extent to which Councillors who are not LDPers can actually share in the exercise of the kind of power that a committee chairman might be expected to have. First, the LDP controls a majority on each committee's directorate. *Riji* can thus control the committee chairman. Second, the LDP always has managed to retain the chairmanship of the more important committees for itself. Currently for example, the Cabinet, Finance, Budget and House Management Committees are all chaired by LDPers. Nonetheless, there is at least some sharing of legislative control with Opposition party Councillors.

This is not the case in the House of Representatives, except with reference to the Special Committees, all but one of which have non-LDP chairmen (see Table 15). All standing committee chairmen in the House of Representatives, however, are drawn from the majority party. Their selection has become ever more deeply enmeshed in intra-LDP factional politics as is readily apparent in Table 16.

[1] Interview with Masaki Yoshiaki, Komeitō — Member of the House of Representatives, in his office 3 July 1970. While his was the most pungent comment, its general tone was reflected in the comments of nearly all interviewees, who were drawn from a broad spectrum of parties and factions.

Table 13   House of Councillors Committee Chairmen in the 1973 Diet session

Committee	Chairman	District	No. of times elected	Background	Party–faction
Cabinet	Takada Kōun	Kumamoto	1	Welfare Min. bureaucrat	LDP – Fukuda
Local Admin.	Kujino Kentarō	Tokushima	1	Prefectural Assemblyman	LDP – Miki
Judiciary	Abe Ken'ichi	Tokyo	1	Business exec.	Komeitō
Foreign Affairs	Hirashima Toshio	Miyazaki	1	S. Manchurian RR. official	LDP – Tanaka
Finance	Fujita Masaaki	Hiroshima	2	Businessman	LDP – Ōhira
Education	Nagano Chin'yu	National	1	Buddhist official (Nishi Honganji)	LDP – Fukuda
Social-Labor	Yayama Yūsaku	Okayama	2	District Assemblyman	JSP – Sasaki
Agric.-For.-Fisheries	Kamei Zenshō	National	1	Food rationing official	LDP – exKōno
Commerce and Industry	Sada Ichirō	Gumma	2	Construction Co, executive	LDP – exKōno
Transportation	Osada Yūji	National	1	Telecommunications specialist	LDP—Tanaka
Communications	Sugiyama Kentarō	Niigata	2	Trade union official	JSP – Sasaki
Construction	Sawada Masaji	Akita	2	Trade union official	JSP – Eda
Budget	Ōtake Heihachirō	National	3	Communications Co. executive	LDP – Fukuda
Audit	Naruse Banji	Aichi	4	Parliamentarian	JSP – Sasaki
House Mgt.	Kurihara Yūkō	Shizuoka	2	Agric. Fed. official	LDP – exKōno
Discipline	Yamada Tetsuichi	National	2	Party official	Komeitō

Summary: LDP 10 (ex-Kōno 3, Fukuda 3, Tanaka 2, Ōhira 1, Miki 1); JSP 4 (Sasaki 3, Eda 1); Komeitō 2.
Source: Based on material in Kokkai Binran [Diet Handbook] August 1972.

Table 14 *House of Councillors Special Committee Chairmen in the 1973 Diet session*

Committee	Chairman	District	No. of times elected	Background	Party–faction
Coal policy	Matsunaga Chūji	Shizuoka	3	Agric Fed. official	JSP – Eda
Ecology	Ōya Tadashi	Hokkaido	1	Trade union official (coal)	JSP – Eda
Traffic safety	Tokano Takeshi	Tochigi	3	Professor	JSP – Eda
Price problems	Yamashita Harue	National	2	Women's Fed. official	LDP – Fukuda
Election system	Kobayashi Kuniji	National	1	Agric.-For. Min. bureaucrat	LDP – Miki
Okinawa and N. Islands	Hoshino Jūji	Yamanashi	1	Agric Fed. official	LDP – Fukuda
Science and technology	Shibuya Kunihiko	Aichi	2	Chief of Research Institute	Komeitō

Summary: LDP 3 (Fukuda 2, Miki 1); JSP 3 (all Eda); Komeitō 1.

Source: Based on material in *Kokkai Binran* [Diet Handbook].

Table 15   House of Representatives Special Committee Chairmen in the 1973 Diet session

Committee	Chairman	District	No. of times elected	Background	Party-faction
Disaster countermeasures	Ishino Hisao	Ibaraki 2	8	Trade union official (Hitachi)	JSP – Peace Comrades
Election system	Tanaka Ei'ichi	Tokyo 1	6	Metropolitan police official	LDP – Ishii
Science and technology	Ohara Toru	Hiroshima 1	6	Trade union official	JSP – Eda
Coal policy	Tashiro Bunkyu	Fukuoka 2	4	JCP official	JCP
Ecology	Sano Kenji	Toyama 2	6	Trade unionist Pref. assemblyman	JSP – Sasaki
Price problems	Yamanaka Goro	Iwate 1	6	Professor JSP official	JSP – Eda
Traffic safety	Kubo Saburo	Ibaraki 1	6	Trade unionist (RR. workers)	JSP – unaffiliated
Okinawa and North. Islands	Asai Yoshiyuki	Osaka 2	3	Pref. assemblyman	Komeitō

Summary: LDP 1 (Ishii); JSP 5 (Sasaki 1, Eda 2, Peace Comrades 1, Unaffiliated 1); JCP 1; Komeitō 1.

Source: Based on material in *Kokkai Binran* [Diet Handbook].

Table 16   *House of Representatives committee chairmen in the 1973 Diet session*

Committee	Chairman	District	No. of times elected		Party-faction
Cabinet	Mihara Asao	Fukuoka 2	4	Prefectural assemblyman	LDP – Mizuta
Local administration	Uemura Sen'ichiro	Aichi 5	5	Lawyer	LDP – Nakasone
Judiciary	Nakagaki Kunio	Aichi 4	9	Parliamentarian	LDP – Ishii
Foreign affairs	Fujii Katsushi	Okayama 2	5	Prefectural Assemblyman	LDP – Miki
Finance	Kamoda Soichi	Saitama 3	6	City Mayor	LDP – Funada
Education	Tanaka Masami	Hokkaido 3	7	M/P admin. asst. parliamentarian	LDP – Fukuda
Social and labor	Tagawa Sei'ichi	Kanagawa 2	5	Asahi newspaperman	LDP – Nakasone
Agric. for. fisheries	Sasaki Yoshitake	Akita 1	5	S. Manchurian RR. official	LDP – Ōhira
Commerce and ind.	Urano Sachio	Aichi 4	5	Prefectural assemblyman	LDP – Ōhira
Transportation	Ihara Kishitaka	Ehime 2	7	Businessman Pref. assemblyman	LDP – Tanaka
Communication	Kubota Enji	Gumma 1	5	Pref. assemblyman	LDP – Fukuda
Construction	Hattori Yasushi	Nara	5	Pref. assemblyman	LDP – Ōhira
Budget	Nemoto Ryūtarō	Akita 2	10	Professor, Ag. For. Min.	LDP – Tanaka
Audit	Utsunomiya Tokuma	Tokyo 2	9	Writer – critic	LDP – Miki
House mgt.	Kaifu Toshiki	Aichi 3	5	Parliamentarian	LDP – Miki
Discipline	Waseda Ryuemon	Aichi 2	12	City assemblyman-parliamentarian	LDP – Fukuda

Summary: Fukuda 3, Ohira 3, Miki 3, Tanaka 2, Nakasone 2, Mizuta 1, Ishii 1, Funada 1.
Source: Based on material in *Kokkai Binran* [Diet Handbook].

The lineup of standing committee chairmen reflects, just as clearly as does the Cabinet, the balance of factional forces inside the LDP, with the larger factions each receiving about three chairmanships and the smaller factions no more than one apiece. Prime Minister Tanaka only placed two of his followers among the chairmen thereby allowing him to reward his allies (Ōhira: 3, Miki: 3, Nakasone: 2), or to encourage his erstwhile foe Fukuda to join the coalition by rewarding his faction with three. By contrast, former Prime Minister Satō, after having been in power for five years, could afford to reserve six of these posts for his own followers in the 1969–70 session of the Diet.

Having proper factional affiliations and the support of one's *oyabun* (boss) are not the only criteria for becoming a chairman. A certain amount of seniority – the average is now five terms – is a prerequisite. Prior service in another representative assembly also has its rewards. For example, the three chairmen drawn from among Mr Fukuda's faction – generally conceded to be the bastion of ex-bureaucrats – all had such prior careers; the same is true of the three drawn from the Ōhira faction, another of those generally classified as part of the ex-bureaucrats' wing of the LDP. Expertise in the committee's sphere of jurisdiction is not among the significant determinants.

These committee chairmen come and go with each new Cabinet or after each new election for the House. While technically appointed by the Speaker or President,[1] they are merely executing the dictates of their party's leaders among whom the faction leaders loom large. All this being the case it may therefore be readily understandable why a chairman of a standing committee in the Diet is almost never able to carve out an independent fiefdom for himself as has been so frequently the case in the American Congress. It has also effectively undermined the intentions of those who sought to institutionalize certain Congressional practices in a Japanese setting. To put it more positively, the process of selecting standing committee chairmen has assisted in adapting and naturalizing an alien import to Japanese circumstances.

None of this should be interpreted as denigrating the powers of a committee chairman *vis-à-vis* the members of his committee. He has an impressive panoply of authority. He determines the date and time of meetings and the length of a hearing or committee session; he may attend meetings of other committees to present his views; he has disciplinary powers over his committee's members, including ordering

---

[1]HR Rules, Chapter I, Article 15; and HC Rules, Chapter I, Article 16, *The National Diet*, p. 67 and pp. 113–14 respectively.

any member who engages in delinquent behavior (as defined by the chairman) to leave the room; he — and only he — has the authority to admit or expel outsiders from an open committee meeting.[1]

A committee chairman is supposed to exercise these powers 'after consultation with the committee', but this legalism is sometimes overlooked. During the hearings of the Special Committee on the Japan — Korea Treaty, for the observation of which the chairman had granted me permission to be an observer, he exercised his powers to terminate committee deliberations in a decisive manner. In the midst of a question being asked at considerable length by a Socialist, the chairman recognized a fellow Liberal-Democrat. He in turn — as quickly and as loudly as his vocal chords would permit — made a complex motion. No one, including the committee scribes, could hear the content of Mr Fujieda Sensuke's remarks because of the pandemonium that prevailed in the room. After the meeting was over the official determination was that the motion had included the following points: that the committee end its deliberations, that the committee approve the treaty and related legislation, that the chairman transmit the committee's decisions to the plenary session for its information. The chairman, who also could not possibly have heard what his colleague had said, ruled that the motion was approved. Obviously, the chairman had not 'consulted' his committee in making his determination; it had all been arranged beforehand in consultation with his party's leaders.

As a consequence of this and similar episodes, committee chairmen — most particularly if they are LDPers — tend to be viewed as agents of the governing party rather than as guardians of a committee's prerogatives to consider legislation that has been placed before it for deliberation. Furthermore, these virtually dictatorial powers that a committee chairman can exercise when the need to do so arises, that need being determined for him by his party's leadership, also help to explain why so many Members of the Diet perceive their work as committee members to be an exercise in futility. In spite of this feeling, the committee structure is elaborate; the committees themselves have extended meetings; Cabinet Ministers must attend when called upon to do so; and experts are required to testify. All this and more, the committees are empowered to do by the Diet Law,[2] but their authority is a chimera and their accomplishments largely meaningless.

[1] HR Rules, Chapter VII, Section 2, Articles 66—75; and HC Rules, Chapter VII, Section I, Articles 38, 42—7, 49—52, and 57—8, *ibid.*, pp. 78—9 and 199—22 respectively.
[2] The Diet Law, Chapter V, Articles 40—52, *ibid.*, pp. 33—7.

Each of the Diet's committees has a relatively substantial staff, despite its lack of impact on the substantive content of legislation that is placed before it. A Specialist (*Semmon-in*) supervises the work of six or eight researchers (*Chōsa-in*) for each committee. Many of the Specialists are drawn from among the ranks of the senior bureaucrats of the Ministry, the jurisdiction of which is the subject matter of the committee. Thus, the Foreign Affairs Committee of each House usually will have an official of the Foreign Ministry in charge of its Research Room (*Chōsa-shitsu*), the Education Committees from the Ministry of Education. They provide the committee to which they are assigned with expert assistance, but they also contribute to the pervasive influence of the national bureaucracy in the operations of the Diet.[1]

Each of the two chambers of the Diet also has a substantial Secretariat in addition to the research staff assigned to each committee. It is headed by the *Jimu Sōchō* (Secretary General) who also serves as the parliamentarian of the House. He is assisted by a deputy and a staff that is divided into seven bureaus each having at least four sections. Each House also has its own Legislative Reference Service (*Hosei-kyoku*) with five bureaus. Additionally, the Members themselves have access to the growingly impressive National Diet Library, right next door to the Diet building.[2] All of these services exist to assist the Representatives and Councillors to fulfill their legislative obligations.

All of these officials – particularly those in the Secretariats – contribute importantly to the smooth functioning of the Diet's machinery. They cannot, however, do very much to increase the influence and power of individual parliamentarians or of the Diet as an institution. This is not to denigrate their efforts, but rather to emphasize that it is the majority party which is in control. It is the Liberal-Democratic Party – so long as it retains its majority – which controls the Cabinet which in turn controls the Ministries and other Agencies of the Japanese Government where the real spade work of legislation is accomplished.

The Secretariat of each House and the research staff of each committee may labor mightily to keep the internal wheels of the Diet in

---

[1] For career details of *Semmon-In* [Specialists], please see any issue of *Shugiin Yōran* [Diet Directory]. This point was also brought up during the course of my interviews with Mr Ogyū and his associates in the House of Representatives Secretariat's Committee Bureau.

[2] Each issue of *Kokkai Binran* [Diet Handbook] provides a complete listing of major officials in the Secretariat, the Legislative Reference Service, and the Diet Library. In the August 1972 issue of *Kokkai Binran*, please see pp. 192–8.

motion, but the energizing power for the whole enterprise is to be found in the endless corridors of the Ministries, Liberal-Democratic Party Headquarters and the offices of the LDP's factions. So long as the Liberal Democrats retain their control of both Houses of the Diet, and so long as factional strife within the party remains within acceptable limits — that is, does not lead to a party split — the LDP can accomplish virtually anything it wants to in the Diet. It can be an awesome process.

CHAPTER FOUR

Diet scenes and confrontations

Shortly after midnight on a Friday morning in mid-November 1965 the Members of the House of Representatives were wearily assembling in the lobbies outside their main chamber. They had been in almost continuous plenary session for three days and two nights. Another — and yet another — all-night session loomed ahead. Lack of sleep exacerbated the prevailing mood of tension.

Fearing that the Liberal-Democrats were planning to trick them by calling for a sudden vote on the Japan—Korea normalization treaty, Socialist Party representatives were alert when the Diet guards opened the doors leading into the Chamber. They dashed inside and formed a cordon around the Speaker's rostrum in order to prevent him from taking his seat and opening the session. The majority party members, however, entered in a slow and dignified fashion, settling in at their desks with apparent unconcern over the antics of their Opposition; senior Liberal- Democrats, sitting in their customary places towards the rear of the chamber, were overheard to remark that their party's leardership had failed them by subjecting them to another sleepless night.

Somewhat non-plussed, the Socialists reluctantly left the rostrum and filed to their seats, assuming their fears to be ill-founded and anticipating continuance of the discussion over a no-confidence motion against Minister of Justice Ishii Mitsujirō. The motion had been introduced by the Opposition as a delaying tactic, and it had been left in abeyance when the recess was called. A weary calm having settled over the assemblage, guards opened the door behind the Speaker's rostrum and Speaker Funada strode into the chamber to take his seat. As if at a signal three groups of relatively young and husky Liberal-Democrats rushed to block the steps leading up to the presiding officer's pulpit to protect him from an Opposition onslaught as Funada began to speak.

Pandemonium broke out as, in a few terse sentences the Speaker announced that he was altering the agenda, that the item of business before the House was the treaty establishing diplomatic relations between Japan and the Republic of Korea and related domestic legislation, that discussions over the treaty were thereby terminated, and that all those approving the treaty should so indicate by standing. By this time nearly everyone was on his feet, shouting in anger, relief or despair. So great was the din that the scribes could not hear Speaker Funada's words. Nonetheless, the official Diet Record dutifully reproduces a transcription of the motions that had been made. It also records that Speaker Funada had introduced the treaty, terminated discussion, and had the treaty approved by what passed for a standing vote, all in less than one minute. That action ended thirteen years of controversy.[1]

While extraordinary, similar scenes of confrontation have taken place on a number of occasions in the Diet over the last quarter century. Why? The basic reason undoubtedly is the deep schism between the majority Liberal-Democrats and their fractured Opposition, especially the Socialists and the Communists. This division in outlook has been especially profound in the field of foreign policy. In a real sense the confrontation of two political and philosophical systems abroad, as exemplified by the 'Cold War', was felt as if it were part of Japanese domestic politics. When an LDP foreign policy position encouraged the alliance with the United States under the auspices of the Security Pact, for example, the Socialists and Communists would counter with suggestions of neutrality or even alliance with the People's Republic of China or with the Communist Bloc in its entirety, in accordance with the vicissitudes of the 'Cold War' and its concomitant international stresses. Similarly, attempts by the LDP to re-establish diplomatic relations with South Korea, excluding North Korea, were perceived by the Opposition as just one more link in the chain entangling Japan in America's fate. Relations, they argued, should be established with both North and South Korea or, if a choice between the two must be made, with North Korea.

[1]*Kampō Gogai* [Diet Record Extra]. 12 November 1965, p. 159. It notes that the plenary session began at 00:18 and ended at 00:19. I had the opportunity to observe Diet proceedings regarding the Japan—Korea Treaty throughout the fall of 1965; details of the events leading up to the final midnight session were obtained during the course of a lengthy interview (on 4 December 1965, in his Diet office) with Mr Tamura Hajime (LDP), who was the organizer and leader of the three groups of LDPers who provide the protective cordon around the Speaker. It is to be noted that no second to a motion is required by Japanese rules of parliamentary procedure.

Discord also plagued attempts to resolve difficulties that might appear to be domestic matters. Two of these were the turmoil in the universities and the problem of how to cope with it. Just as the government party opted for an alliance with the United States, so the students wanted to show that they were emulating the Cultural Revolution in China in the late 1960s. They occupied campus buildings for months on end, subjected professors to 'accusation and self-reflection' sessions often lasting for fifteen to twenty hours at a time; disrupted faculty meetings by a variety of techniques including locking up the faculty and only permitting limited food or drink to reach the prisoners; reduced classes to a shambles by shouting through loudspeakers in the courtyards or singing and banging on walls in the hallways – it was a lively scene, and one which, despite a respite at the outset of the 1970s, may be starting again.

The resolution of the problem once again pitted the government party against the Opposition. The Liberal-Democrats decided to have the Ministry of Education draft a stern bill. Entitled the University Temporary Management Measures Law, its major provisions were designed to allow the Minister of Education to take over a university that had been in the midst of serious turmoil or had not functioned as an academic institution for several months; also, the designation of a university as non-functioning was itself to be made by the Minister. In the Socialists' view this solution negated the principle of university autonomy, hallowed in post-war Japan as one of the pillars of democracy. President of the House of Councillors Shigemune took matters into his own hands in a manner similar to that of Speaker Funada in the case described above. That is to say, in order to ensure that the Liberal-Democrats in his chamber could add their approval to the bill, President Shigemune – without warning – revised the day's agenda and called for a vote on the bill.[1] It was approved.

One factor contravening traditional parliamentary norms in the Diet is, as seen above, ideological – the profound differences in international and national society – that become manifested by hard positions on legislative proposals. A second factor is organizational – the internal structure of the LDP and those of its Opposition parties.

---

[1] HC Rules, Chapter VIII, Section 2, Article 88. 'When the President recognizes it necessary, or when such a motion is made by a Member or Members, the President may alter the order of the agenda or add other bills or matters to the agenda by referring it to the House to decide upon . . . without debate.' *The National Diet*, p. 134.

One of the requirements imposed by factionalism is that a party's position be determined by lengthy debates among the groups within a party. In the case of the governing party, it means long discussions involving Ministerial bureaucrats, members of the LDP's Policy Research Council (*Seimu Chôsa-kai*), and faction and party leaders.[1] Similar negotiations must be conducted among JSP officials, or between them and other Opposition party colleagues if a united campaign against the LDP is to be agreed upon. In this complex process, promises of a firm stand for or against a measure are made to the various parties' supporters who are outside the Diet and with whose expectations a Representative or Councillor cannot trifle if he desires to be re-elected. All of this means that party positions — at least for public purposes — become fixed.

Another factor becomes significant at this point: the concept of compromise is not valued highly in Japan; being 'sincere' and 'pure' — that is to say, not deviating from a principled position — are the qualities of character which are much admired. Thus, public deviations and discussions are permissible only before consensus with the ranks of one of the antagonists has been reached. After its consummation, party discipline (the German expression *Parteizwang* carries more punch and is more accurate than the pallid English) is imposed. The consequence of this is the virtual absence of public inter-party debate. Representatives and Councillors expound positions in accordance with their parties' edicts; inevitably, it is almost pure chance if the phrases uttered by one side bear any resemblance to those spoken by the other. Any meaningful negotiations among antagonists in the Diet must therefore take place behind closed doors or the Diet would be a constant scene of disorder. This it is not.

Perhaps a lesser reason than the ideological, structural, and value-oriented factors promoting scenes of confrontation in the Diet, but one which is often a catalyst to the others, is that of time — or the lack thereof. Concurrent votes in both Houses determine the length of a Diet session, although the Diet Law requires that an ordinary one (*tsūjō*) last for 150 days.[2] All parties agreed that the extraordinary session convened in the fall of 1965 to consider the Japan—Korea Treaty

---

[1]Haruhiro Fukui, *Party in Power: The Japanese Liberal-Democrats and Policy-Making* (Berkeley and Los Angeles: University of California Press, 1970); and Thayer, *How the Conservatives Rule Japan*, provide a wealth of material on this topic.

[2]Diet Law, Chapter 2, Article 10, *The National Diet*, p. 27.

should last for 70 days. That length would provide some leeway between its closing (on 23 December) and the opening of the next ordinary session scheduled by law to begin each year during the final ten days of December unless special circumstances arise such as the holding of a general election.

Seventy days would seem sufficient for legislative action to be taken regarding one item of business, even a major one. To be sure, Liberal-Democrats also planned to have the Diet approve certain much-needed supplementary appropriations to the budget, but it was the approval of the international agreement that was accorded first priority. For the LDP, one additional time constraint was salient: Articles 60 and 61[1] of the 1947 Constitution provide that a decision reached by the House of Representatives will prevail if it has been made 30 days prior to the end of a session regardless of what action is or is not taken by the House of Councillors. This provision is operative only with respect to the budget and treaties. For Prime Minister Satō—who was staking his political future on the treaty's approval – this meant that the effective period of time available to the Representatives to approve the treaty was not 70, but only 40 days.

The Socialists were publicly committed to block the treaty, but it was generally conceded that the best they could do was to slow down the legislative process. They realized that, barring some *deus ex machina*, their prospects for accomplishing their stated goal were minimal; the LDP had the votes, roughly three to two among the Representatives and four to three among the Councillors. The Socialists also were aware that nothing they said in committee meetings or plenary discussions would influence their antagonists. The LDP's leadership had arrived at a consensus and the Prime Minister could be expected to make certain that discipline would prevail, especially since he was still consolidating his power base within the party; he was in the first of his seven years

[1]'The budget must first be submitted to the House of Representatives . . .

Upon consideration of the budget, when the House of Councillors makes a decision different from that of the House of Representatives, and when no agreement can be reached even through a joint committee of both Houses, provided for by law, or in the case of failure by the House of Councillors to take final action within thirty (30) days, the period of recess excluded, after the receipt of the budget passed by the House of Representatives, the decision of the House of Representatives shall be the decision of the Diet . . .

The second paragraph of the preceding article applies also to Diet approval required for the conclusion of treaties.' *The National Diet*, p. 15.

of office. Hence, the only possible course for the Socialists to prove to their supporters that they had given their all to prevent the successful following of Satō's timetable was to force the LDP into extending the length of the session – at least once, and – if possible twice.[1] Doing so would not prevent the Diet's approving the treaty, but it would demonstrate their sincerity.

It is difficult to frustrate the will of a determined majority in the Diet. Tactical devices are minimal in number. Control of the calendar is in the hands of the majority through its control of the presiding officers, a majority of each House Management Committee, and at the committee level through the fact that a majority of each of their directorates is LDP, even though the chairman may occasionally be a member of the Opposition. All of this taken together prevents the pigeon-holeing of a legislative measure unless the LDP is willing.

An old-fashioned American Senate-style filibuster cannot be mounted. 'The President of each House may limit the time for questions, debate, and other speeches, unless otherwise decided beforehand by the House.'[2] Additionally, each chamber's 'Rules' enable twenty Members to introduce a motion to shut off further discussion. Discussion of the foregoing motion can be limited to two Members for and two against and a motion to end that discussion can be made by 20 Members. The presiding officer puts the last motion to the House 'without debate'.[3] Talking has limited utility as a delaying tactic.

Ōno Bamboku, a colorful former Vice-President of the LDP, is credited with the invention of one dilatory device. It was during the Occupation era and the foreign tutors were trying to have the Diet approve a bill nationalizing Japan's coal-mining industry. Ōno, a man of long experience in representative assemblies, having been a Tokyo City Assemblyman before entering the House of Representatives, utilized one ingenious line of conduct to oppose the measure. He organized a select group of his fellow Liberal Party Members to prolong the taking of an open ballot. Voting in either House can be either by rising at one's desk, or by casting ballots. Each Member has a stack of hard plastic

---

[1]Diet Law, Chapter II, Article 12, 'The term of a session may be extended when both Houses agree by their concurrent vote.'

'The extension of the term of a session shall not be made more than once for an ordinary session and twice for a special session or extraordinary session.' *Ibid.*, p. 27.

[2]Diet Law, Chapter VI, Article 61, *ibid.*, p. 40.

[3]HR Rules, Chapter VIII, Section 4, Articles 140–2; and HC Rules, Chapter VIII, Section 4, Articles 111–13, *ibid.*, p. 93 and p. 137 respectively.

chips at his desk, white (for) and blue (against). Officials of the House Secretariat have receptacles into which the Members deposit their white or blue chips. Separate containers are provided for each color ensuring that the balloting is open and easing the task of counting. These containers are placed on the raised dais which is located immediately below the presiding officer's chair, leaving only a rather narrow passage through which the Members walk while casting their ballots.

No time limit is specified in either the Diet Law or the Rules of the respective Houses governing the taking of a formal ballot. Thus it has happened that this process has required as much as three hours to complete, when it can be accomplished in fifteen to twenty minutes if conducted at a normal pace. Dilatory voting has acquired a special name: *gyūho senjutsu*, literally 'cow-walking' but usually translated as 'snail's pace tactics'. It can be temporarily effective.

Enacting this stratagem takes place under different circumstances in the two Houses. Opposition Representatives vote first in that chamber. This permits them to converge on the narrow passageway through which all must pass to deposit their ballots. They can do so as soon as the clerk of the House has begun to read the roll. Once they reach the ballot boxes, they merely stand there instead of casting their votes. In doing so, they consciously create a traffic jam that rivals the kind that occurs at the junctions of Tokyo's expressways where four divergent streams of traffic are expected to merge into two narrow lanes. LDPers are faced with a human wall that will only gradually give way. Inevitably there is a good deal of pushing and shoving. As tempers rise, injuries can be sustained. On one occasion I witnessed a Socialist receive a minor cut on his hand in such a scuffle. Immediately, his comrades joined him in raising a terrible din. Doctors were called for and efforts were made to halt the plenary session altogether. Speaker Funada, backed up by the Liberal-Democrats, would have none of it and the balloting continued at an even more unbearably slow pace. Most Members exercise extraordinary self-restraint. Quite possibly this is because a secret understanding has been reached beforehand that the delay will be conducted for an agreed-upon length of time after which — the necessary points having been scored — the proceedings can resume at their normal pace.

In the House of Councillors, it is the majority party's Members whose names are read first. Consequently, their ballots are cast with alacrity, but the oppositionists cast theirs in an agonizingly desultory fashion. They will arise from their seats, take a step or two, stop to chat with a colleague, carefully examine some of the magnificently ornate wood-work that decorates the chamber, finally reach the ballot boxes only to discover that they have forgotten to bring along a chip, or perchance that they have carried one of the wrong color. They must retrace their steps with extreme deliberateness, and do anything except deposit their ballot. All the while, the President is periodically inquiring whether anyone present still desires to vote. Once he has heard the inevitable chorus of 'Ayes', he will intone the phrase '*tōhyō onegaishimasu*', 'please cast your ballots'.

Tensions rise and dispositions become sour, understandings to the contrary notwithstanding. Patience is needed for the majoritarians not to push too hard in the House of Representatives, or not to shout excessive encouragement to their dawdling colleagues in the House of Councillors. Doing so might precipitate a real brawl, which would merely serve to delay proceedings more. By the same token, the Opposi-tionists must have the courage of their convictions and at least some physical strength to conduct their stand-in and to withstand the deri-sive comments that are shouted at them; there is always the pos-sibility of being made to appear foolish either to the observers in the visitor's gallery or the much larger audience that is watching the proceedings on television. It may all have become as ritualized as the delicate and subtle movements of a *Nō* dance-drama; even so, to be executed stylishly, ritual requires rigid discipline; and that necessary discipline sometimes breaks down in the heat generated by a confronta-tion. In the final analysis 'snail's pace tactics' (*gyuho senjutsu*) have become accepted. They constitute one of the few viable devices of delay.

Motions of no-confidence are a second device. They can be intro-duced against the entire Cabinet, against a Minister, the presiding of-ficers, and the Chairman of a standing or special committee. All that is required is for twenty Members to submit a petition setting forth their reasons. They are normally accorded precedence over all other business before the House; this by custom rather than any legalism.

Considerable amounts of time can be consumed in disposing of no-confidence motions. First, there must be an agreement on how much time will be devoted to proponents and opponents of the motion. Demands that each of the housekeeping decisions be made through casting of formal ballots must be honored so long as twenty Members present the demand. In turn, snail's pace tactics can be utilized in each of these procedural motions. All except the last minute of the three-day, two-night plenary session ostensibly devoted to a discussion of the Japan–Korea Treaty was absorbed by consideration of motions of no-confidence against various Cabinet Ministers and the Chairman of the Special Committee that had been established to review the treaty and related domestic legislation. Of course, it was the last minute that counted.

At one point in the session the Cabinet Minister against whom a motion of no-confidence had been introduced and discussed and was being voted on found it absolutely necessary to leave the chamber. His departure added a completely unintentional element of delay. All doors of the chamber are locked while a formal ballot is being taken, and no one is allowed in. To make his hurried exit the Minister had to receive special permission from the chief parliamentarian. Having departed, he was not able to return; yet, custom commands that the individual against whom a no-confidence motion is being considered be present in the chamber. A raucous and uncontrollable discussion ensued. How could the vote on the motion continue when the individual concerned was not present, and how could he be in attendance when no one is to be admitted until the vote is completed? Speaker Funada could do nothing except call for a recess to untangle the parliamentary snarl. The majoritarians lost precious hours, while the minoritarians relished the delightful delay.

At the final midnight meeting three days later the Liberal-Democrats managed to retaliate against their opponents by the simple device of altering the agenda. The Socialists had every reason to believe that discussion regarding the no-confidence motion against Minister Ishii Mitsujirō would continue; after all, such motions are supposed to have preference. This, however was a miscalculation on the part of the JSP, which learned that not at all times do motions of no-confidence receive preferential treatment. Still, they do have their uses in postponing the inevitable for the Opposition; for the majority they are a nuisance which can be tolerated so long as it finally triumphs.

Occasionally, certain tactics of delay that are employed by the Socialists do cross that imprecise border which is drawn between near-violence and the thing itself. In the spring 1960 Diet during which the revised Security Pact with the United States was approved the bonds holding the Japanese parliamentary system together came perilously close to being snapped. The Speaker was imprisoned in his office so that he might not be able to be in his chair to open the plenary meeting. Corridors in the Diet building were blocked by Socialist Representatives and their assistants. In the end, Speaker Kiyose had to telephone the Metropolitan policy to enter the Diet Building itself to break up the sit-in. Policemen, who are to be distinguished from the regular Diet guards,

had to drag the Oppositionists from the scene one by one.[1] Simultaneously, thousands of demonstrators were milling about in the Diet
compound. Some were so infuriated by the prospect that the treaty
would be approved that they urinated against the main doors leading
into the central hall of the Diet. That entrance is usually reserved for
the Emperor. Those scenes were not part of a ritualistic exercise.

Events of May—June 1960 have left an indelible memory in the
minds of those who are Members of the Diet, its Secretariat, and the
forces of law and order. In the interim the Diet compound which used
to be easily accessible has become a kind of fortress, especially when the
Diet is in session and a controversial item is on the agenda. A high
fence now surrounds the compound and the *kido-tai* (riot police) who
have become extremely well-trained in calibrating their riot control
techniques from gentle firmness through whiplashing brutality are
always ready to respond to the slightest inkling of a disturbance. A
Japanese newspaperman in reflecting on it all one day a decade after
the trauma of 1960 told me, 'No one had anticipated the intensity of
the pent-up emotions which were unleashed.'[2] Memories of those
events have played a consequential role in delineating the kind of conduct that is permissible within the Diet and of its immediate environs.

Liberal-Democrats have counte ed those Opposition tactics of delay
which are prompted by despair with one principal device. Its use
contributed to the Socialists' willingness to resort to tactics of confrontation, especially such admittedly non-parliamentary behavior as
locking up the Speaker. *Kyōkō Saiketsu* is the phrase that is used by the
Japanese to describe what occurs. '*Saiketsu*' means nothing more than
'taking a vote' or 'division of the House'. The dictionary translation for
'*kyōkō*' is 'force' or 'enforcement'. Japan's English language press
translates this phrase as a 'forced vote', which carries with it the implication that the parliamentary whip is making the rounds insuring
that his party members will be present for a crucial roll call and
that they will vote in accordance with the 'party line'. That is not what
a 'forced vote' means in Japan.

Kyōkō Saiketsu is the majority party's taking into its own hands the
entire procedural machinery for running the Diet's internal affairs. In

---

[1]For a complete description, please see George R. Packard III's superb
Protest in Tokyo, The Security Treaty Crisis of 1960 (Princeton University
Press, 1966), *passim.*, but especially pp. 234—42.
[2]The comment was made in confidence.

so doing, the majority LDP's leadership consciously ignores the procedures that exist to insure the participation of the Oppositions: the various parties' Diet Strategy Committees (*Kokutai*), the respective House Management Committees (*Giun*), meetings of the parties' Secretary-Generals and of the supreme party leaders, and all the provisions in the Diet Law or the Rules of the respective Houses specifying that a presiding officer (Speaker, President, Chairman of a Committee) shall make certain procedural rulings only after consulting the membership of the House or a committee. Oppositionists, principally the Socialists, refer to all of this as exemplifying the 'tyranny of the majority'.

When Speaker Funada altered the agenda, in the scene which opens this chapter, he did not do so 'after consulting the House without debate'.[1] To have done so would have eliminated the element of surprise that the Liberal-Democrats felt they needed in order to achieve treaty approval speedily enough to avoid a major riot. It was also argued that inasmuch as the LDP had an absolute majority in the House they would therefore have won a vote on a procedural motion 'consulting the House' in any case, and that therefore such consultation was superfluous. Earlier in the same Diet session Ando Kaku, who was the Chairman of the Special Committee on the Japan—Korea Treaty, used the same prerogatives to end committee deliberations by recognizing a fellow LDPer in the midst of a Socialist's question. President Shigemune of the House of Councillors employed the same tactic in ramming the University Law through.[2] In that instance, the Councillors' Standing Committee on Education had not devoted even one minute of discussion to the proposed bill before taking a 'forced vote' which approved the bill and sent it on to the plenary meeting for its disposition.[3] Use of such tactics may require that the most visible actor, generally the presiding officer, resign his post and tender his official apologies to all concerned before the Opposition will once again be willing to participate in the parliamentary process.

Sometimes excessive use of the 'forced vote' can have more funda-

---

[1] HR Rules, Chapter VIII, Section 2, Article 112. 'When the Speaker deems it necessary, or upon a Member's motion, he may alter the order in the agenda, or add new items to it after consulting the House without debate.' *The National Diet*, p. 89.

[2] HC Rules, Chapter VIII, Section 2, Article 88, *ibid.*, p. 134.

[3] Please see my 'An Aspect of Japanese Parliamentary Politics', *The Japan Interpreter*, Vol. VI, No. 2, Summer 1970, pp. 196—205.

mentally adverse repercussions. During the Security Pact crisis days of 19—20 May 1960 — it was another midnight session which was central — Prime Minister Kishi, by utilizing the *Kyōkō Saiketsu* technique over and over again (in the Special Committee; in the House Management Committee; in the Diet in order to stop the legislative clock, to extend the length of the session, and to ram the treaty itself through), brought not only the Diet into turmoil.[1] Outside the Diet these moves became the focal points for the largest mass demonstrations in Japanese history. Inside the Diet they created a shambles of the legislative process. In the LDP, they assisted in triggering a revolt of some factions against their party President, namely Prime Minister Kishi himself. He had restricted his consultations regarding the tactics that were to be used to those factions which were in his mainstream coalition, leaving even many LDPers in the dark as to what was to transpire. This deliberate oversight was critical. It might be permissible for the LDP to force the Opposition to its will, but it must be accomplished in a manner not impairing unity within the majority party — if one wishes to continue as party President—Prime Minister. It is in this context that the constraints imposed by factionalism become operative in limiting the LDP leadership's potentially authoritarian tendencies.

Matsumura Kenzō, a former Minister of Education, had run against Kishi in the January 1959 LDP Convention for the post of party president. His faction was led jointly by him and Miki Takeo, who later was to become one of Satō's Foreign Ministers and Deputy Prime Minister under Tanaka. Matsumura's candidacy had had the support of the factions led by Ishibashi, who had been Kishi's immediate predecessor and who had to retire prematurely because of ill health, Ishii Mitsujirō, who was later to become Minister of Justice and Speaker of the House of Representatives, and — most important of all — Ikeda Hayato, who was to succeed Kishi as LDP President and Prime Minister.

These leaders and their factional followers were not convinced that Kishi's handling of the Security Treaty imbroglio had been as adept as it might have been. They criticized his parliamentary strategy on the basis of a distinction which is more a matter of style or attitude than one which is absolutely clear. In Japanese, this contrast is referred to as being the difference between *kō-shisei* (high posture) and *tei-shisei* (low posture). Under Prime Ministers Kishi and his younger brother

---

[1]Scalapino and Masumi, *Parties and Politics in Contemporary Japan*, and Packard, *Protest in Tokyo*.

Satō Eisaku, LDP voices who favored a 'high posture' have tended to prevail. They believe it is the LDP's duty to use its power to push its legislative program through the Diet so long as the Japanese voters provide the LDP with a working majority. Furthermore, they contend that the Oppositionists — especially the Socialists — have been so 'un-Japanese' in their policy orientations that they can and should be ignored with impunity.

Their LDP opponents who controlled the party under Prime Minister Ikeda (his faction is now led by Foreign Minister Ōhira Masayoshi) tended to espouse the benefits of a 'low posture.' Its components include not pressing too hard for policies or legislative programs that are known to be anathema to the Opposition parties; not to rely on the excessive use of the 'forced vote'; and to stress what at the time were non-controversial goals such as an ever-expanding GNP under the income-doubling program pushed by Ikeda in the early 1960s. For them, speedy Diet approval of highly controversial pieces of legislation was less important than giving the highest possible priority to the preservation of parliamentary procedures in accordance with the Diet's Rules. To do so requires endless discussions, negotiations, and allowances for the Opposition to use every parliamentary device at its disposal to procrastinate; but, in the final analysis, they contend that only in this fashion can the Diet and parliamentarism survive in Japan. Furthermore, this style is more in accord with the traditional Japanese method for reaching a decision, that is, by maximizing consensus.

Not long after the House of Representatives' forced vote approving the Japan—Korea Treaty Mr Ōhira who had served as Ikeda's Foreign Minister and who later served in the same role for Tanaka, but who was not a Cabinet Minister at the time ruminated about the parliamentary strategy that Prime Minister Satō had employed in that instance. He commented that if he had been writing the script for that session (as he had done so effectively for Ikeda), he would have recommended one additional step. Approach the Socialists with the promise to allow one extension of the Diet Session — for example ten days — in return for a promise by the Socialists to tone down and limit their obstructionist tactics. He believed that such an agreement could have been negotiated. It would have allowed the Socialists to approach their public supporters with a partial victory, 'You see, our tactics succeeded in forcing the LDP to extend the Diet session'; and it would still have resulted in the treaty's being given the Diet's seal of approval. Furthermore, it would all have been accomplished in a much more dignified fashion and avoided another shock which would add to the public's disenchantment with the Diet.[1]

LDP high posture hawks respond that consultations with the Oppositionists can lead to a slowing down of the entire governmental process and eventual immobilism. To succumb to that siren song would be equivalent to the majority party's abdicating its responsibilities for governing Japan. Mr Fukuda Takeo who is a close associate of former Prime Minister Kishi, a former Foreign Minister, and subsequently Minister of State but was not in any of Mr Ikeda's Cabinets summed up his feelings regarding the low-posturists with the statement: 'Prime Minister Ikeda is the worst prime minister of the worst cabinet of the worst government in the world.'[2] Participants in intra-LDP politics obviously take the *kō-shisei* — *tei-shisei* distinction very seriously.

Disagreements over parliamentary tactics also exist within the Socialist Party. One of the major reasons for Nishio Suehiro's faction's defecting from the JSP and establishing the Democratic-Socialist Party was the — to them — fundamental issue of parliamentarism. Should Socialists seek to achieve their goals within the framework of electoral contests and legislative political processes or should they rely on violent action? Nishio and his immediate followers responded unequivocally in favor of parliamentary politics; some JSPers tried to find a middle ground which would not lead to an outright break-up of the party by fuzzing up the issue (Kawakami Jōtarō, who was JSP Chairman in the early 1960s and whose personal commitment to parliamentarism was unquestioned, found himself in that unenviable position); and some militants in the Sasaki faction and the Heiwa Dōshi-kai (Peace Comrades' Association) maintained that the forces of capitalism would never submit peacefully to their goals, thus making violent action an absolute necessity.[3]

The Democratic-Socialists under Nishio and his successors as party chairmen, Nishimura Eiichi and Kasuga Ikkō, have persevered in their

---

[1]Interview with Ōhira Masayoshi (LDP), in his Diet Office 26 November 1965.

[2]Interview with Fukuda Takeo (LDP), in his home 9 July 1963 during the course of a *yo-mawari* (night rounds) in the company of about ten Japanese newsmen. I still recall my surprise at the vehemence of Mr Fukuda's remarks.

[3]The most complete study analyzing these issues is Allen B. Cole, George O. Totten III and Cecil H. Uyehara, *Socialist Parties in Postwar Japan* (Yale University Press, 1966). Please see especially pp. 85–114.

commitment to parliamentary politics; but the DSP's influence is declining. It would be incorrect to infer a cause and effect relationship between the DSP's espousal of parliamentarism and its decline in popularity except in one respect. This is that in acting as the parliamentary voice of conscience in the Diet it has been perceived as being less firm in its opposition to the LDP than the more aggressive Socialists. A similar problem has been posed for the other centrist party, the Komeitō. Until the 1972 election it had been making spectacular advances. There had thus not been any reason for Komeitō Members to question the validity of their tactics in the Diet: oppose the majority LDP, but in a restrained and selective fashion. Both the DSP and the Komeitō are faced with a dilemma. How does one make oneself heard and one's influence felt while caught between the LDP's massive majority, the JSP's prestige as the major Opposition party, and the growing power of the JCP? It is a dilemma that neither party has resolved.

This dilemma has been made all the more acute by the Communists having come close to tripling their number among the Representatives (from 14 to 40) in the last (1972) election. If the Communists continue to act non-violently, as they have for over a decade, but are simultaneously able to be the LDP's most vigorous and effective opponents in the Diet — a role that they are capable of playing — it is they who will receive most of the headlines and the credit with that portion of the public which is tired of LDP government.

A great deal of the future prospects for parliamentarism hinges on the tactics of the JCP. If it restricts itself to non-violent competitive politics, the other Opposition parties can be expected to follow its lead. If, on the other hand, the JCP provides any evidence of using 'unfair' tactics (as defined by its opponents, especially among the other Opposition parties), then one can anticipate the onset of a vicious cycle of escalating violence with each Opposition party trying to outdo the others in proving that it is the most militant, and therefore most pure, in bringing about the downfall of the LDP, and the LDP in turn responding to those of its own leaders who believe that the only way to deal with the various elements of their Opposition is to crush them.

This bleak prospect is in the realm of the possible. I believe, however, that its realization is unlikely. This belief is supported by some verifiable factors. Foremost among these is the evidence that in all parties, government and Opposition alike, there are elements that are trying to make the Diet work in a non-violent manner. Furthermore, on an individual basis there have been in the past and can be in the future prudential concerns which constrain even the militant forces, thus strengthening the hand of the moderates in keeping certain explosive issues from consideration by the Diet — or in channeling their expression into non-violent forms. On the other hand, profoundly divisive problems can arise not only by intent but also by force of circumstance or tactical miscalculation. The danger lies in the delicacy of the equilibrium, the array of potentially explosive issues that exist in contemporary Japan, and in the severity of the demands for sagacity in parliamentarians who are, after all, human beings like the rest of us.

Neither moderates nor militants are always in control because neither are permanently in positions of leadership in their respective parties. In the LDP there is a constant jockeying for power between those who advocate a high-posture strategy and those who believe that more can be accomplished through pursuing low-posture politics; there is also endless strife within the JSP between the moderates under former Secretary General Eda Saburō and the militants under former Chairman Sasaki Kōzo. The forces can shift toward or away from balance. The Diet functioned quite smoothly and was the stage for only minor confrontations from the summer of 1960 until the fall of 1964, the period during which moderates Prime Minister Ikeda Hayato and Chairman Kawakami Jōtarō lead the LDP and the JSP respectively. On the other hand, the mediators can be overwhelmed; that is what happened in the Spring of 1960. Contributing to that debacle was the legislation at issue — the United States—Japan Treaty of Mutual Security and Cooperation — which had become controversially explosive. This allowed the militants on both sides to win their arguments, to harden their positions, and to constantly escalate violent tactics. Those scenes were not repeated in 1970 when the Pact came up for renewal, but if the LDP 'hawks' had been successful in their advocacy of extending the Pact for a set period of time (five or ten years), which would have necessitated Diet approval, a repetition of the 1960 confrontation would probably have occurred. Instead, those who favored extending the treaty's life through the automatic extension clause were victorious (after ten years the agreement is to continue until a year's notification is given that one of the partners wishes to abrogate it);[1] consequently,

---

[1] '... after the Treaty has been in force for ten years, either Party may give notice to the other Party of its intention to terminate the Treaty, in which case the Treaty shall terminate one year after such notice has been given.' 1960 U.S.—Japan Security Treaty, Article X, Paragraph 2. Packard, *Protest in Tokyo*, p. 367.

those opponents of the pact who had been preparing for the better part of the decade to engage in another major confrontation were deprived of a specific target, and their campaign was limited in its effectiveness. Also, the Japan of 1970 was a different country from what it had been a decade earlier. Its people took pride in the tremendous strides that they had achieved in increasing their gross national product to the third largest in the world. Feelings of frustration were still plentiful — economic expansion had created massive problems of pollution, housing conditions were appalling, public transportation groaned under excessive use, sewerage and waste disposal were inadequate, and a host of other irritations remained — but none of them could be easily employed to challenge the fundamental viability of the political system. However issues with revolutionary potential do exist. The 1960 Security Pact was one. More current is constitutional revision; I am convinced that profound emotions would surface if attempts were made to alter provisions relating to the role of the Emperor regardless of whether the sought-for changes were on behalf of strengthening the imperial institution or abolishing it.[1] The same is true with regard to the 'no war' clause in which Japan renounces the use of force in the settlement of international disputes.[2] This issue includes subsidiary, but equally deeply felt, subjects for dispute such as massive remilitarization leading to the acquisition of nuclear weapons. Memories of the agony and havoc created by the atom-bombings of Hiroshima and Nagasaki remain deeply imbedded, but so do bygone aspirations of imperial glory. There are others. Any expressed need, whether domestically motivated or externally imposed, to fundamentally alter the existing equilibrium would be fraught with the danger of re-energizing latent forces of antagonism and discord.

Should that occur the Diet would inevitably again become the stage for acting out serious confrontations. The mettle of its Members would

[1] The 1947 Constitution of Japan, Chapter I, the Emperor. Article 1, the most important of the eight articles, states 'The Emperor shall be the symbol of the unity of the people, deriving his position from the will of the people with whom resides sovereign power.' *The National Diet*, p. 4.

[2] The 1947 Constitution of Japan, Chapter II, Renunciation of War. Article 9 reads: 'Aspiring sincerely to an international peace based on justice and order, the Japanese people forever renounce war as a sovereign right of the nation and the threat or use of force as means of settling international disputes. . . .

In order to accomplish the aim of the preceding paragraph, land, sea and air forces, as well as other war potential will never be maintained. The right of belligerency of the state will not be recognized.' *The National Diet*, pp. 5–6.

be severely tested as their actions determined whether the Diet would act as a safety valve or a focal point for revolution.

The Diet is, after all, a representative institution. In that capacity it mirrors, with some distortions to be sure, Japanese society. Confrontations in the Diet rarely occur because of personal desire to engage in combat; they occur because the Members feel compelled to act out society's turmoil, for to do otherwise would be breaking faith with those who elected them. My hope is based on the real contribution that the politicians in the Diet make: to translate into symbolic conflict the sources of discord within the society. It is a considerable accomplishment.

CHAPTER FIVE

A tentative assessment

Four marble pedestals stand in the central hall under the dome of the Diet Building. Three of them are occupied by statues of famous Japanese statesmen. In one corner stands a likeness of Ito Hirobumi, the architect of the Meiji Constitution and the first President of the House of Peers. In the second corner there is another bronze statue, that of Okuma Shigenobu, the founder of Waseda University and an early Meiji era oligarch who worked to create a national assembly that would be representative of the Japanese people. On top of the third pedestal is the statue of Itagaki Taisuke, one of the earliest champions of the movement on behalf of popular rights (*Jiyu-Minken Undo*) in the 1870s and 1880s and who was the founder of the first political party in modern Japan.

The pedestal in the fourth corner stands empty, which is conveniently overlooked in the narrative of the book of photographs, *The National Diet of Japan* published by the House of Councillors in 1961. Over the years, the principal candidate to fill the void has been Ozaki Yukio, a champion of parliamentary politics from the turn of the century through the early 1950s. He is remembered in America for having brought the cherry trees to Washington, D.C. while he was Mayor of Tokyo in 1910. His contributions to parliamentarism are preserved in the Ozaki Memorial Hall located within the Diet compound and housing a museum and library about the growth of the Diet in Japanese politics.

Leaving the fourth pedestal unoccupied has other implications. It may reflect the desire to produce art that is asymmetrical, Japanese aesthetic sensibilities are sometimes best served by a feeling of incompleteness. More pertinent may be the belief that the Diet is still maturing and is not yet a full-fledged parliamentary institution. As long as the fourth pedestal remains unoccupied the Members of the Diet and the Japanese public are reminded that much work remains to be done in furthering the efficacy of parliamentarism in their country. This, at any rate, is the reason given during guided tours of the Diet.

In certain respects, the explanation of the empty pedestal symbolizes

121

some of the doubts the Japanese feel about their parliamentary institution. It raises fundamental questions relating to the role that the Diet does play in Japanese politics, and the role that it should play.

It could be argued that the Japanese Diet is the very model of a parliamentary institution. The 1947 Constitution states that 'the Diet shall be the highest organ of state power, and shall be the sole law-making organ of the State'. Both chambers are occupied by representatives of the Japanese people freely elected by all citizens twenty years and older (with minor and inconsequential exceptions). Japan's political party system encompasses a broad spectrum of policies and ideologies ensuring that most — possibly all — segments of society have the opportunity to send their spokesmen to the Diet. Elections to and sessions of the Diet are monitored by one of the most extensive networks of news media in the world; there is little doubt that the people of Japan are fully, but not always critically, informed by their newspapers as well as the public and private radio and television stations, except for certain taboo subjects such as the Emperor. Each of the Diet's two Houses has a full complement of specialized (by subject matter) standing committees that appear to permit careful scrutiny of different segments of the heavy legislative load. There is a plenitude of assistants and staff in each chamber's secretariat: the researchers attached to each committee, the legislative reference bureaus of each House, and the Diet Library professionals who are available to help a Member needing information. Representatives and Councillors receive salaries and the perquisites of office that, while not munificent, are generally considered to be adequate.

Other factors could be mentioned, but even those cited could readily support the conclusion that the Members of the Diet and the institution itself have all that is necessary to be a successful parliament. Such a conclusion is conceivable, but before it is accepted prematurely, it is necessary to discuss in somewhat greater detail each of the descriptive statements that has been made. For, while I would defend their generalized accuracy, they are incomplete and are therefore partially misleading.

The Diet's constitutional role

On paper the Diet is unquestionably the highest law-making organ of the Japanese state. No legislative bill, whether it be entirely new, an amendment to an existing law, a treaty, or a resolution, becomes the law of the land until it has been approved by a majority of members in both Houses (providing there is a quorum in attendance). It is worth recalling that with regard to the National Budget and treaties the will of the House of Representatives predominates if thirty days of a particular session remain.

These constitutional mandates are not to be denigrated lightly. The Diet does act as a kind of sieve sorting out those pieces of proposed legislation that are to be approved from those that are not. It accomplishes this function in an indirect fashion. Most legislative bills — the exceptions are so minor as to be basically irrelevant — originate with the Cabinet. Behind the Cabinet stand both the leadership of the majority party, the LDP, and the vast Japanese bureaucracy.

Typically a bill originates in one of the Ministries. It is then discussed by the Council of Administrative Vice-Ministers, and at the same time is also discussed within the elaborate hierarchy that governs the LDP. At this stage of the pre-legislative process, it is entirely possible that the item under consideration will become involved in intra-LDP factional disputes. One faction might argue that the bill, if presented to the Diet, could result in a serious confrontation with the Opposition, and should therefore be shelved for the time being. Another faction might argue that the bill is of high priority and should therefore be pushed forward at all costs. A third might argue on behalf of strengthening or weakening a particular provision of the bill. While much of this jockeying is hidden from public view, participants in the process have told me that compromises are made. After a consensus has been reached among the senior leaders of the LDP and ministerial bureaucrats involved, the bill is submitted to the Cabinet for its approval. Once it has received the Cabinet's imprimatur, the bill goes to the Diet with the presumed full support of the Government (i.e. the bureaucracy) and the majority party. It must be emphasized that all of this takes place behind closed doors and that access to the proceedings is limited.

In the meantime, the Opposition has been made aware that such a bill is pending or is at least under consideration for submission to the upcoming session of the Diet. Opposition party leaders in turn may well decide that the bill is to be deemed controversial, and that they will make a massive effort to oppose it. Such a decision of necessity also requires arriving at a consensus either among the factions of the major opposition party, the JSP, or among all of the opposition parties, the JSP, Komeitō, DSP, and the Communist Party.

What is important about all of this is that the positions to be taken by the antagonists in the looming legislative battle have been decided before the Diet session has even begun. Furthermore, the attitudes to be voiced by the actors may only have been arrived at after lengthy intraparty factional disputes in the LDP and the JSP or interparty battles. Finally, given the importance that is accorded to the concept of group loyalty in Japanese behavior, any deviation from the commitments made within the ranks of either side is viewed with considerable hostility. In practical terms, this means that there is virtually no room for further compromise or negotiation between the representatives of the majority party and opposition parties. For such negotiation to be meaningful or compromise conceivable, it would be necessary that the positions taken by either of the groups of antagonists must be flexible. Such flexibility, to put it bluntly, is simply lacking. Consequently, the fate of a particular legislative proposal is completely predetermined even before a Diet session begins — assuming that one side has an absolute majority in both chambers, as has been the case for the LDP since 1955.

This cursory summary of the pre-legislative and legislative processes leads to at least one significant conclusion that is to be drawn: the postwar National Diet is just as much of a rubber stamp as the prewar Imperial Diet became in the 1930s. What has changed is the set of forces that operate to control the Diet. In the prewar years it consisted of the military and civilian bureaucracies in conjunction with the large industrial—business interests (*zaibatsu*) that were the motive and determining powers. In the postwar years, while the military bureaucracy has become infinitely less powerful, it is a combination of the civilian bureaucracy together with major economic interests (i.e., the *zaikai* operating through the Keidanren and Nikkeiren) that provide the principal policy input.

The sorting function of the Diet is therefore nothing more than to allow legislative proposals supported by the bureaucracy and vested interests that support the LDP to be approved and to block those proposals which originate from sectors of the Japanese society affiliated with the opposition parties. Japanese intellectuals in their criticisms of the Diet emphasize the image of the parliamentary system as being a handmaiden of 'the establishment'. They also stress the pervasive power of the national bureaucracy because they claim that the Members of the Diet, particularly LDPers, are robots controlled by the bureaucrats. In other words, they assert that the parliamentarians are workers on an assembly line powered by the bureaucracy and the products of this are molded by the bureaucracy in conjunction with business interests which together constitute Japan's ruling elite.

Whether these criticisms are valid depends on what aspects of the legislative process are stressed. Without exception, the Dietmen who were interviewed expressed their concern about the degree to which the national bureaucracy is still almost overpoweringly influential. Without exception, they complained about the extent to which a Cabinet Minister was dependent upon his bureaucratic 'subordinates' and how little Ministers managed to be able to think for themselves.

These criticisms are so much a part of the conventional wisdom about the role of the Diet and of the Members of that institution in the legislative process that it is difficult to argue against them. What these criticisms, however, do overlook is the Diet Members' exercise of judgment which, in the final analysis, may be far more important than the ability to draft a particular legislative proposal in an elegant fashion in conformity with the Japanese version of legalese.

Judgment is, of course, peculiarly difficult as a factor for analysis. First of all it is extremely difficult to measure by comparison with the influence that might be exerted by a group of bureaucrats on a piece of legislation. To measure the latter, all that would be necessary would be to compare the original draft prepared by a bureaucrat with the final version adopted as legislation by the Diet. If the language were similar then one could presume that what counted was the influence of the initial drafter. Secondly, to know exactly where a Diet Member's judgment was crucial, it would be necessary to be privy to the process of drafting legislative bills and to be fully involved at each separate stage of the entire sequence in order to observe the behavior of all of the key actors. Even if one were fortunate enough to have gained access to the inner decision-making processes in order to observe and record the manner in which specific individuals exerted their influence, one would never be absolutely certain that one had seen or heard the crucial point at which influence was exerted or judgment exhibited. After all, that may well have taken place during the course of a telephone call rather than at a formal meeting of the Cabinet, a faction, or a full meeting of the Policy Board (*Seichō-kai*) or Executive Board (*Sōmu-kai*) of the LDP, or whatever.

Nonetheless I would submit as a hypothesis that the leaders of the major political parties do exercise judgment. It is they who make the choices of which bills to push forward and which to be given a lesser priority; it is they — if they are in the opposition — who determine to what degree a proposal made by the majority is or is not to be made controversial and the extent to which various devices or tactics of delay are to be employed. It is regrettable — at least from the perspective of gaining an understanding of what transpires — that so much of this very crucial portion of the legislative process takes place in a manner that is hidden from external observation. It is also regrettable that that which does transpire in public is nothing more than the playing out of a script that has been written beforehand and that the observable actors are merely reading lines or obeying the directions of playwrights who may not even be present for the final act of their dramatic production.

What takes place on the public stage of the Diet, whether it be in committee sessions or in plenary meetings, is the majority party's having its way. There is within the framework of the system very little room — if any — for compromise, so that amendments of any significance that are sponsored by the Opposition to a legislative proposal made by the Cabinet and supported by the majority party have little chance of being adopted. For that to take place it would be necessary for a split to have occurred in the ranks of the majority party. So long as such a split does not take place — and it has rarely happened since the LDP was organized in 1955 — the opposition parties may question, they may harass, they may utilize every device of delay available to them, but in the end the LDP's will prevails. It is this hard wall of reality that has to be faced by anyone who would see the Diet as being something more than just a rubber stamp for the majority party's overwhelming power. Nonetheless, it is to be noted that those who write the script for a particular Diet session do so with the knowledge that a proposal will or will not have relatively smooth sailing and thereby influences the manner in which the script-writers set forth their schedule. It is the exercise of this judgment which does allow the Diet and its members to play a significant role in the legislative process and which enables them to exercise their prerogatives of being members of the highest law-making institution of the Japanese Government. Thus, the Diet and its elected inhabitants do live up to their mandate, but they do so only in a severely limited and indirect fashion.

Political parties and elections

Japanese elections are free according to the usual criteria for such contests: all adults have the right to vote, and the voters have a choice beyond merely voting 'yes' or 'no' for a specific slate of candidates. Furthermore, over the years since the Second World War there has been extraordinarily little violence during elections, and there has been no exaction of penalties levied against voters who supported candidates of parties or groups that might be considered outside the broadly defined mainstream of Japanese electoral politics. Finally, the spectrum of parties appealing for the public's support is quite broad, ranging as it does from some fringe ultra-nationalistic groups on the extreme right to the Japanese Communist Party on the left. Some university students are involved in what in Europe have been termed 'extra-parliamentary opposition' activities, but their influence seems to be waning from the high-water mark reached during the heady pseudo-revolutionary fervor that gripped Japan's campuses in the latter half of the 1960s.

There is little doubt that the Japanese voter does have a choice and that he can exercise it freely. Nonetheless, Japanese critics of the system do have some complaints about the degree to which the electoral system as it currently operates results in the Members of the Diet — in their totality — accurately reflecting the views of the Japanese public, assuming of course that such representation of different segments of the public is at all possible. (One can argue that the whole concept of representation is chimerical.)

Critics contend that the electoral and party system does not result in an accurate representation of the Japanese public — and its various segments — for a number of reasons. First, they assert that the electoral contests are too expensive, and that this gives an undue and unnecessary advantage to candidates with larger sources of funds available to them over those whose political funds are more limited. In 1969, for example, the monthly pay of members of the Diet was Y320,000 (at the then exchange rate, about $900.00). By contrast, Japanese newspapermen estimated that a successful candidate would need about Y100,000,000 (about $280,000.00) for his campaign, and that one who spent only Y70,000,000 (about $200,000.00) might well be defeated. These estimates of expenditures vary widely from those which are reported under the requirements of the Japanese Political Funds Contribution Law, which is normally referred to as being made in the shape of a bamboo sieve (a *zaru-hō*). Even if one should concede that these estimates of needed campaign funds are inflated, it is nonetheless generally accepted that to run for a seat in the Diet is an expensive proposition. This is not to imply that Japanese electoral contests are rampantly corrupt, meaning that there is outright vote-buying. What it does imply is that those segments of the public which are in a position to make substantial financial contributions to candidates do tend to have more influence with the elected representatives than do those who are not in such a position. Furthermore, it reduces the potential independence of the elected representative by virtue of making him dependent not only on his party but also — at least in the cases of the

LDP's and JSP's candidates — on financial campaign aid from one of the party's 'bosses' (*oyabun*). The voter may be free in making his choice, but the choices with which he is faced have not necessarily been freely determined. That is to say, that the elected representatives may consider themselves far more beholden to those who made substantial financial contributions to their campaigns than to the average voters in their districts.

A second general criticism leveled at the electoral system is that there is an unnecessarily large difference among the sizes (as measured in population) of the electoral districts. Generally, the LDP has benefited from the advantage of the rural as opposed to the urban voter and is a direct consequence of the Occupation's Land Reform program. Tenant farmers who acquired ownership of their land have become staunch supporters of the *status quo*. It is therefore not likely — so long as the LDP remains the majority party — that these imbalances will be corrected in any fundamental manner.

A third criticism is one that is directed at the multi-member district system. In the House of Representatives, Japan is subdivided into 124 electoral districts, each of which with one exception returns three, four or five candidates to the Diet. One might suppose that this multi-member district system allows candidates of the opposition parties to have an advantage in that the available pool of voters who are dissatisfied with the *status quo* is larger. In a sense this is true, but it would be truer if the opposition parties could concentrate their energies on behalf of mutually agreed-upon nominees. Instead, each normally runs its own candidates so that the 'opposition' vote is splintered. The Komeitō and DSP on the one hand, and the JSP and JCP on the other, made some efforts to jointly back one candidate in certain districts in the 1972 election. It was not very effective as a solution. By contrast, the LDP has been far more successful in endorsing just the correct number of candidates in order to maximize the electoral impact of its available popular vote in the district.

Endless discussions by Diet Members, bureaucrats and academicians have taken place as to how the existing district system might be improved. These range from the creation of single-member constituencies through prefecture-wide constituencies to a combination of party list together with single-member districts. What is noteworthy is that the LDP's managers have understood how the existing system can be made to work to their candidates' advantage far better than the strategists of the opposition parties, except for those of the Komeitō whose political sagacity has rivalled that of the LDP, prior to 1972.

Both of these criticisms have contributed their consequential share to the belief that even though the Japanese political party and electoral system is free it is not necessarily fair. In turn, this belief has allowed critics of the Diet to claim that although public opinion on a particular issue or policy may be pointing in one direction, the majority of votes cast in the Diet are at variance with the desires of the public. This point was frequently made — especially in editorials — in connection with the Japanese Government's policy of maintaining formal relations with Taiwan rather than with China prior to Prime Minister Tanaka's decision to journey to Peking in September 1972. That is to say, that the LDP which was the governing party of Japan in the 1960s was pursuing policies that were contrary to the will of the public as articulated by the media, that therefore the Diet was not a truly representative institution.

This and similar disparities between what certain segments of the public believe should be Japanese policy and what the majority in the Diet enunciates and supports as official Japanese policy has also led to the growth of some splinter radical student groups that believe that the whole parliamentary system is a sham and that some system of extra-parliamentary rule should be established. In a curious way their attitudes partially reflect some of the same kind of anti-parliamentary bias that was displayed by the more militant young army officers in the 1930s. They, too, believed that the party politicians in the Diet did not reflect 'the true will of the Japanese people' and that they should therefore be superseded.

For the time being, a repetition of the events of the 1930s that led to the dissolution of political parties and the turning of the Diet into a rubber stamp of a self-appointed 'elite' is relatively remote. Its relative unlikelihood should not blind us to the potential hazards that certain imbalances in the system as it currently operates do present. Atavistic nativists periodically assert that the mystical essence (*kokutai*) of the Japanese state is wrapped up in the imperial institution. Radical student revolutionaries are even more vociferous in maintaining that the elect-oral process and the party system merely obscure and obstruct the mystical forces of history as divined by the leaders of the working class. No matter how wrong-headed and out of place in contemporary Japan one might believe these very different but equally mystical visions to be, they feed upon and are fueled by any real or perceived inequities of the system. Especially is this the case among the Japanese people, whose reputation for stoicism is as well known as their volatile shifts in mood are misunderstood and unanticipated.

Information and the media

The Japanese people have entered the communications era with an excellent network of news media. There are three very large national newspapers — the *Asahi,* the *Mainichi* and the *Yomiuri,* and several medium-sized national papers such as the *Sankei,* and the *Nihon Keizai.* Additionally, several weeklies such as the *Asahi Journal* and monthlies (*Chuo Koron, Bungei Shunju*) frequently publish serious political analyzes in their articles. Electronic media include the two T.V. channels of the publicly-owned Japan Broadcasting System (NHK), and several private broadcasting networks each of which has television and radio stations. While most of them concentrate on national and international news — thus helping to create an integrated national outlook — some local subsidiaries do provide coverage of provincial happenings, and the national dailies have one or two pages devoted to 'local' news. By and large, however, it is nation-wide issues which are emphasized.

All of them provide their readers or listeners with an almost incessant stream of political news and commentary. Each of them has a large reportorial staff so that it is possible for journalists to become specialists in the most minute aspects of their particular beat. Consequently, some of their commentary is so filled with technical jargon that it is incomprehensible to the average reader.

So pervasive is the influence of the media and their representatives that one of the most commonly debated topics is whether it is the Government which rules Japan or the media which control the formally appointed or elected presumed masters of the country. In the autumn of 1972, for example, it was the media which fostered a 'mood' among the public on behalf of having a general election for the House of Representatives. During the summer and early fall Prime Minister Tanaka had repeatedly asserted that he would not call for a dissolution of the House of Representatives and a new election. In the end, the Prime Minister gave in to 'public opinion', as shaped by the media. Furthermore, by focusing the public's attention on a particular policy issue or by emphasizing certain proceedings in the Diet the media help to determine the public's view of the operations of their Government.

Some parliamentarians are not altogether satisfied with the amount of coverage that their activities receive. It is not so much that they dislike exposure — much of it is extremely beneficial by the time the next election takes place, since it contributes to voter familiarity with their names, in turn adding to the advantages that an incumbent enjoys. Rather, instead of concentrating on the issues under discussion at a particular meeting, some Members find themselves — or worse, their colleagues — unable to resist the temptation of playing to the large gallery that might be observing them via the magic of 'living color' screens at home.

It is to be noted in this connection that plenary session and committee meetings are open to the press and the all-seeing eye of the television cameras if permission is granted by the presiding officer concerned — i.e. Speaker, President, or Chairman of a committee. Refusals are so rare that I am not aware of any. All of this coverage could be interpreted as constituting nothing more than a barrage of propaganda dulling the senses and critical faculties of any who would read or listen. Given the generally critical tone *vis-à-vis* the Government and the LDP of the major newspapers and networks, it would be very misleading to assert that the press is a rigid handmaiden of the powers that be in the manner of the prewar era. Actually, the exact opposite criticism has been leveled against the media by many individuals including former Prime Minister Satō. In his farewell press conference before leaving office, Mr Satō lashed out at what he perceived to be his tormentors in a manner reminiscent of Mr Nixon's 'You won't have Dick Nixon to kick around anymore!' outburst after his loss in the California gubernatorial election of 1962.

Despite the overall critical stance and depth of coverage that have become the hallmarks of Japanese journalism, some problems are present. Possibly most serious is the 'press club' system. A reporter may receive an assignment from his editor to cover the Diet. In order to fulfill his mission he must also be permitted to join the Diet's press club, which is not an association for pursuing the better things in life, but is a kind of guild. To remain as a member of the 'club', he must observe certain unwritten rules such as not scooping his colleagues. If he should do so in the name of competition, he might face the prospect of expulsion from the club and the consequent inability to fulfill his assignment. Additionally, it would be considered unwise to write stories that are constantly critical of those who control the flow of information from the institution he is assigned to cover. To do so might impair his access to background briefings and the subtle guidance without which it becomes difficult to make sense out of what he has learned. In other words, the rules of the reportorial game must be understood if one is to retain credibility with those who furnish the information that one needs.

To survive in this system a reporter quickly learns that certain kinds of criticism of men, institutions or policies are permissible but others are not. None of it is codified, but it is certainly intuitively felt. For example, at the time of the so-called 'black mist' (*kuroi kiri*) scandals in 1966, 'political desk' reporters who had long known something was amiss fed their information to Socialists and reported the resultant Diet interpellations in their newspapers. Simultaneously, the alleged malfeasances were being exposed by reporters from the 'social desk', which is comparable to the city desk in American newspapers and has very little to do with the activities of the jet-setting 'beautiful people'. Social desk reporters cover natural disasters and crime, so that they are in fairly close and constant contact with the forces of law and order. As such, they would not be compromising their access to privileged sources of information by blowing the whistle on certain important political figures in contrast to their political desk brethren. This is an example of the influence of taboos and illustrates the subtle distinctions between what is and what is not 'reportable'.

What all this really adds up to is that despite the fullness of the information that the press makes available to the Japanese people, on some occasions some of the most crucial elements of the story are not fully told. It has frequently been my experience to learn more during a fifteen-minute conversation with a practising journalist than in weeks of poring over Japanese newspapers and magazines. It is not that there is outright suppression of news, or even an undue amount of pre-censorship and/or self-censorship — although there is some — but rather that, especially as an outsider, one needs help in learning to read between the lines and in gaining an understanding of what is really salient and worth knowing. In this respect it is not only foreigners who are the outsiders.

One further aspect of the media's performance in the Japanese political process is crucial. Both foreign and domestic analysts of Japanese society have commented on its apparent compartmentalization. In her model of Japanese society Professor Nakane Chie of Tokyo University has stressed its hierarchically organized and segmented structure that emphasizes vertical rather than lateral communication. This picture of Japanese society leaves open the question of what kinds of ties — if any — bind the society together; that is, what is it that provides the cement which keeps the separate compartments from falling apart into a pile of rubble. After all, most foreign commentators tend to emphasize the nearly monolithic unity of purpose in their perceptions of Japanese behavior.

The media of communication play a vital role in informing different sectors of the society of what others are doing or are thinking of doing.

This generalized information dissemination function is, of course, a normal feature of the functions performed by the media in non-totalitarian systems. In Japan, its practitioners go one step further. Newsmen are vital links between different compartments of 'influentials' in Japanese society.

To illustrate: As noted previously each reporter is given a particular beat, whether it be the Prime Minister's Office, the Foreign Ministry, the Diet, LDP or JSP Headquarters or whatever. Some of them, beyond covering their official assignment, become affiliated on a personal basis with an important personage in Japanese politics. Hence, though one's official duty might be to write up the day's news from 'X' Ministry, one's unofficial but possibly more crucial obligation would be to maintain close ties with a LDP factional leader who at that moment is serving as Chairman of the party's Policy Board.

A newsman who has such dual affiliations will at the end of his day's official assignment quite frequently visit his private patron later in the evening during the course of his 'night rounds' (*yo-mawari*). He will not be alone in doing so, as there will be newsmen from other major dailies or the television and radio networks. The senior political figure who is serving as host will provide a variety of refreshments, and there will be a relaxed conversation during the course of which significant bits of information and reactions thereto will be exchanged and disseminated. From the host's point of view these sessions allow him to learn what has been transpiring in other factions of his party, the opposition parties, the Government, etc. in a fashion that is far more informative than were he to read the relevant stories in the next day's morning edition of any of the major dailies. From the newsman's point of view, these sessions allow him to probe for possible reactions of his host concerning certain developments that have taken place or are projected — i.e. whether smiles of approval or an impenetrable mask greet his revelations. For an outsider like myself it was not always easy to comprehend the cryptic comments that were bandied back and forth (on those occasions that permission was granted for me to attend) until I was able to ask about the significance of this or that item. Nonetheless, I am convinced that these late evening private talk shows provide some of the key links in overcoming the compartmentalized character of Japanese society. The *yo-mawari* provide bridges for the flow of information across what ordinarily appear to be chasms of non-communication between different segments of the nation. It also provides a safeguard against most threats to impose a blanket of permanent secrecy over important affairs of state. Of course, it must be realized that the entire Japanese public is not immediately informed, but rather that the circle of those who are gradually well-informed is enlarged.

Inherent in the system of the *yo-mawari* and the patron-client relationship which it symbolizes is a certain loss of independence on the part of the journalist. It is entirely possible that a newsman can become so beholden to his patron that he becomes a spokesman for that faction leader — so much so that the newsman in effect becomes a member of that faction, and has thereby lost his capacity to be an autonomous practitioner of his craft. By itself, the workings of the Japanese media, including such elements as the *yo-mawari*, would be an interesting subject for systematic scrutiny. On the basis of my own all-too-limited experience I would maintain that whatever dangers might be present in the (possibly excessively) close ties between a politician and his client reporters are offset by the greater circulation of what might in others systems be deemed private or confidential. In other words, it enhances rather than reduces the flow of information, but more among the ranks of the elite than within the public at large.

Diet organization and committees

The standing (subject-matter) committee system is probably the least successful postwar innovation in the internal organization of the Diet. Available evidence suggests that this committee system was introduced by the Occupation to create autonomous centers of power inside each chamber of the Diet. As was noted in Chapter 3, it was the Congressional model that was the basis for the reform undertaken by the primarily American Occupation officials. While this Congressional committee model was reproduced in form its substance has not been transplanted; nor, quite possibly, should it have been.

There are a number of reasons for this divergence between form and substance. First, the Diet is still under the dominance of the executive (i.e. the Cabinet), which uses the mechanism of its control over the majority party to determine what does and does not happen in all nooks and crannies of each chamber. Constitutionally it is the Diet that elects the Prime Minister, but this is a formality since the real decision has been made at the LDP Convention at which the party president has been elected. It is he who selects the members of the Cabinet — keeping in mind the requirements for factional balance so that the party does not fragment — and (formalities to the contrary notwithstanding) it is he in conjunction with other senior LDP leaders who selects all the standing committee chairmen in the House of Representatives and also those in the House of Councillors, with the exception of the few opposition party chairmen in the latter chamber.

Formally speaking, the Cabinet is collectively responsible to the Diet. In practice, so long as the majority party retains its majority and does not splinter, the Cabinet is in a controlling position. Inasmuch as committee chairmen owe their appointments to the Prime Minister and, to a lesser extent, their faction leaders, who put forth candidates for consideration, they are highly unlikely to exercise their powers independent of the wishes of the party's directorate. Furthermore, since the committee chairmen control what transpires in their committees, aided by the committee's *riji-kai*, or board of directors, which is also dominated by majority party members, the expectation that committees could become independent centers of power just cannot be considered fulfilled nor even probable of fulfillment barring unforeseen circumstances.

Membership on a committee does allow one to become more familiar with certain spheres of governmental policy, or provides opportunities for raising questions of Cabinet Ministers and other Government officials who appear before the committee. In this sense, committee hearings provide for the dissemination of information to a broader public. This facet of committee activity is potentially influential outside the Diet on a particular piece of proposed legislation or public policy. The potentiality may be present, but it is rarely made manifest because government spokesmen evade the substance of the question. Even if the question is answered fully, the impact on the passage or non-passage of legislation remains minimal so long as the majority manages to hang together in its support of the legislative proposals.

Generally, Members of the Diet denigrate the committee stage of deliberations. LDPers tend to perceive it to be a nuisance and a waste of time since substantive decisions have been made already. Members of the opposition parties are frustrated by the knowledge that even though committee hearings permit them to delay the LDP from exercising its will, the deliberations themselves have little impact — if any — on the shape of the proposed bill or governmental policy. In short, there is a high level of dissatisfaction by all concerned regarding the Diet's committee system.

Despite this bleak picture, it is likely that the present committee system will not be altered in the foreseeable future. This conclusion is based on a large number of discussions with Dietmen who, after having vented their frustration with the *status quo*, were shocked to hear me ask, 'If the committees are really that useless, why not abolish them altogether?' Somehow this question triggered consternation; possibly (though this hypothesis is as yet untested) because an affirmative response might indicate that Members of the Diet had not learned all there is to be known about the workings of a parliamentary institution. Furthermore, while committees may not be autonomous actors on the stage of the Diet, they too must be taken into account by those who write the script for a legislative session. This does have the effect of enlarging the number of individuals whose views must be taken into account in formulating Diet strategy. Hence, while committees may not be independent, their existence cannot be entirely ignored. From this perspective, the functioning of Diet committees may be considered marginal in the legislative process, but perhaps even a marginal role is better than none at all.

Staff assistance

Enlarging the staff available to each Member of the Diet, providing each committee with specialist research assistants, and increasing the overall size of the Diet Secretariat that supports the work of each chamber, as well as creating the nucleus of a documentary, newspaper, journal and book collection that ultimately has become the impressive National Diet Library, all of these efforts which were undertaken during the years that Japan was occupied were intended to strengthen the capacity of the Diet and its members to acquire greater autonomy.

These efforts rested on the assumption that an informed membership of the Diet could more effectively challenge the bureaucracy's expertise. It is an assumption that is open to doubt. An excessive amount of information can serve to inhibit the capacity of a Member to see the outline of the proverbial forest instead of being submerged in the shadow of a mass of trees. Members have complained that they and their colleagues have been trying to acquire expertise in the minutiae of legislative proposals rather than concentrating their energies on the 'large picture'.

As noted in Chapter 3, the Diet's capacity to act autonomously is not precluded by a lack of staff assistance. Instead, one element of the problem is that the available staff is not entirely responsible to the Diet. Its budget is largely determined by the Finance Ministry, as is true for all other segments of the national government. Furthermore, especially with regard to the specialist staff that is available to each committee, many come on temporary loan from the Ministry the work of which that committee is supposed to monitor. Aside from that, the contest for influence is unequal between the expertise that is available within the national bureaucracy and that which is available to Members of the Diet. In order to make it equal either the size of the staff available to the Diet would have to be increased to match that inside each of the ministries, or the bureaucrats would have to feel a very deep sense of commitment to the belief that the Diet is in fact supreme. Neither of these conditions prevails.

The governing majority party — i.e. the LDP — can and does rely on the ministerial bureaucrats to provide expert assistance or policy proposals. There is a fairly constant and high level of consultation between bureaucrats and counterpart segments of the LDP's Policy Board. Hence, the Secretariat and the committee staff more often than not serve the research needs of the opposition Members than they do the needs of the majority Members who do not really need it anyway. Inasmuch as the majority party — together with the Finance Ministry, of course — controls the purse strings by virtue of being charged with the adoption of the budget, the officials in the Secretariat cannot be too enthusiastic in their assistance to opposition Members. To do so in a fashion that would effectively challenge the capacity of the LDP to push through a bill might well result in the demotion of the official concerned or his being labeled as not quite reliable and hence not to be considered for advancement to a position of greater responsibility and trust.

It may well be that the expectation of the foreign occupiers who relied on the Congressional model attempted to reproduce within the framework of a parliamentary system something that could not be made to work. It is well known that inside the American Congress each committee and, more importantly, each committee chairman tends to have a good deal of autonomy *vis-à-vis* either the House or the Senate and *vis-à-vis* the executive branch of the government. Inasmuch as committee chairmanships are decided on the basis of seniority, it behooves the staff members of a committee to be on reasonably good terms with the committee chairman or the ranking minority Congressman or Senator on whom they are dependent for their position.

None of this holds true in the Diet. Committee chairmen come and go, usually in conjunction with each Cabinet change, and committee staff are not dependent on the committee members — senior or otherwise — for their promotions. This is in no way to denigrate the work that is done by the Diet Secretariat or the specialist staff of each committee. They work hard in assisting the Members of the Diet, and without them it is entirely possible that the Diet's machinery would cease to function.

But the inescapable conclusion is that increasing the size of the staff and research facilities which have been made available to the Members of the Diet has not notably enhanced the capacity of the Diet to act autonomously.

Salaries and perquisites

Members of the Diet receive salaries equivalent to the highest paid career officials (administrative vice-minister) in the bureaucracy. In 1969 it was raised to Y327,000 per month (under the new exchange rate, slightly in excess of $1200.00), which by Japanese standards is by no means a paltry salary. Nonetheless, it is not sufficient to permit a Member to consider himself free from financial worries.

As noted, electoral campaigns are extraordinarily expensive. Costs vary in accordance with the size of the district, how long one has been in office, how well one's support groups (*kōen-kai*) are organized and other variables. Costs of campaigning are generally high enough to make it impossible for the vast majority of candidates to finance their own campaigns. Inevitably, this means that a candidate becomes dependent — to some degree — on those who helped him financially.

Once one has been elected, there are numerous other expenses which have to be met. Unless one's district is in the immediate environs of Tokyo, it might be necessary to find a residence in the capital — in itself a substantial financial burden. Constituents may come for a visit, and at a minimum this will involve the expense of a lunch but very possibly far more, such as providing a tour of the city in a chartered bus or even paying for the overnight lodging of one's supporters. To do otherwise is to court the risk of defeat in the next election.

How individual Dietmen manage to make their financial ends meet is a murky and quite delicate matter. Even though they enjoy more or less unlimited franking privileges to communicate with their constituents, and even though they are the beneficiaries of such other perquisites as free passes on the national railways, it all does not help very much to meet the expenses involved in assuring one's longevity as a Member of the Diet.

Few have no economic anxieties. It is in this connection that the role played by a faction leader in the LDP or the JSP becomes crucial, for without his beneficence, which in turn is dependent on his capacity to raise funds from various sectors, most Members simply could not keep their personal accounts in the black. Sometimes the roles between faction leader and follower are reversed. Current Prime Minister

Tanaka was able to become an important leader inside former Prime Minister Satō's faction partially because he is extraordinarily energetic, but also because his own wealth and his ability in fund-raising helped keep the Satō faction afloat.

In this respect too, therefore, the capacity of an individual Member to act autonomously — and as a consequence the capacity of the Diet's entire Membership to do so — is severely circumscribed. For this situation to be altered either all Members would have to be independently wealthy and thereby not in any sense representative of the Japanese public, or the expenses involved in running for office and staying there would have to be substantially reduced. Neither alternative is believed to be plausible.

Financial constraints contribute to the maintenance of discipline among a party's members and help to reduce any tendencies towards independent behavior. Both of these consequences place severe limitations on the capacity of Dietmen to conform to an imaginary ideal of independent legislators assiduously cultivating the fertile fields of law-making. Admittedly, such an ideal is far-fetched for a number of reasons previously alluded to. More importantly, however, the Members' collective financial worries render them dependent on those of their supporters who can assist them financially or on their patrons, thus limiting any proclivities they might have had to respond to the wishes of their electors in an even-handed fashion. That objective, which is implicit in the better salaries and enlarged perquisites, remains unfulfilled.

Conclusion: the roles of the Diet

In the end we must return to the fundamental question. What role or roles does the Diet actually play in contemporary Japanese politics? Formally, the Diet lives up to its Constitutional mandate. No other institution or group of individuals has challenged the constitutionally grounded supreme prerogatives of the Diet. It is of course conceivable that there will be another 'restoration' of the Emperor and the Imperial institution — as some of those who favor amending Article I of the new Constitution propose; but this has not occurred yet and is generally believed to be unlikely barring a fundamental shift in attitude among the Japanese people or a majority of their political leaders.

Nonetheless, categorically to assert that the Diet is, as the Constitution puts it, 'the sole law-making organ of the state', is to obscure rather than to illuminate the roles that the Diet as an institution and its

139

Members do actually perform. The Diet and its Members ratify or approve decisions the substance of which have been made elsewhere. The House of Representatives has the final word in electing the Prime Minister, who, of course, is Japan's chief executive; but that decision — in substantive terms — has been made by the Liberal-Democrats assembled in convention. Formally, the Diet may enact laws; but the substance of this legislation was drafted in final form elsewhere, primarily by the bureaucrats. The Diet may be said to approve international agreements formally entered into by Japanese Government representatives; but again their substance was drafted outside the halls of the Diet.

If all this is the case — and the available evidence tends to support these generalizations — would it then be justifiable to conclude that the Diet is no more than a cypher in contemporary Japanese politics? Such a conclusion, though fashionable, is as inaccurate as the argument that the Diet's role is entirely in conformity with its Constitutional prescription.

One compelling reason negates the concept of the Diet as an absolute nullity. Substantive decisions, to be sure, are made outside the Diet, but if they are to be effectuated (i.e. generally accepted as being legitimately a part of the law of the land) their proponents must take into account the balance of political forces present in the Diet at a given point of time. This balance reflects — possibly not completely and possibly in a somewhat skewed fashion — the political forces that are significant. If there is a deep division among the public concerning the 'correct' policy that Japan should pursue *vis-à-vis* China, or the United States, or the Soviet Union, then an international agreement that Japanese officials might enter into with any of these countries' officialdom will create serious problems inside the Diet. If there is a deep division within Japanese society over the functioning of their universities, legislation dealing with them — as drafted by the Ministry of Education bureaucrats — will also have to take into account that this societal lack of consensus will be reflected among the Members of the Diet who are constitutionally required to approve such a bill before it becomes a law.

If, then, the Diet's most crucial role is to reflect the divisions of opinion and the pluralistic groups of the Japanese society, questions can be raised about the accuracy of the mirrored image. Critics may contend that the reflected image of societal forces is distorted in the Diet. It is not so distorted, however, that the Diet has lost its function as the legitimizer of decisions made by the Government. For, despite the serious disturbances that took place in and around the Diet at the time of the approval of the revised Security Pact with the United States in 1960, or at the time of the approval of the treaty re-establishing diplomatic relations with the Republic of South Korea in 1965, or at the time that the Diet approved the University Law in the summer of 1969, once the Diet had acted the issue was resolved for the time being. In so doing, the Diet performed an invaluable role as a safety valve for what might otherwise have been situations with revolutionary potential.

Institutionally, the Diet performs one other function that may well loom as being of even more long-lasting significance. It has become the training ground, or finishing school, for Japan's supreme political leaders. Whatever their prior careers may have been — and one can maintain that there are too many Tokyo University Law faculty graduates, or that there are too many ex-bureaucrats either from government ministries or the trade union movement, or that there are too many businessmen, etc. in the Diet — the fact of the matter is that each of the last three Prime Ministers (Ikeda, Satō and Tanaka) had lengthy careers in the Diet prior to becoming Japan's chief executive. Furthermore, with very few and hence notable exceptions, the overwhelming majority of Cabinet appointees have had at least six terms in the House of Representatives (or about fifteen years of service in the Diet) or two terms at a minimum in the House of Councillors (upwards of twelve years of service). Students of the human psyche might assert that one's character and personality are determined by one's genes or by the traumas of adolescence, but habits of mind and of work cannot help but be influenced to some degree by the institutional setting, especially if a significant span of time is involved. At a minimum this hypothesis is worthy of further exploration.

Finally, as the Japanese themselves begin to accord greater recognition to the fact that a career in the Diet is one major avenue to political influence and power within their society, it might be anticipated that an increasingly larger number of younger men and (hopefully) women will turn to it as an outlet for their ambitions. In the meantime, and so long as a career in the Diet is the prime determinant for achieving political power — as defined by a ministerial appointment to a Cabinet portfolio — the prestige and the influence of the Diet in Japanese politics will remain significant, and may ultimately lead to the Diet's living up to the full prerogatives of its Constitutional mandate.

An introductory bibliography

This bibliographic essay has been prepared to assist those who desire to delve somewhat more deeply into the study of Japan and its domestic politics. It is suggestive and selective and is limited to English language materials, although some items were initially written in Japanese.

Several one volume introductions are useful as points of entry into the study of Japan. Edwin O. Reischauer's *Japan: The Story of a Nation* (New York: Knopf, 1970), and Richard Storry's *A History of Modern Japan* (London: Penguin, 1963) are eminently readable. Both emphasize the last one hundred years. An excellent collection of essays ranging across a broad spectrum of major topics is contained in John W. Hall and Richard K. Beardsley, *Twelve Doors to Japan* (New York: McGraw-Hill, 1965). *New York Times* Tokyo bureau chief Richard Halloran, in his *Japan: Images and Realities* (New York: Knopf, 1969), defines and analyzes some of the glaring contradictions that baffle observers. A beautiful book, with photographs, that has some of the same flavor but is written from an Italian rather than American perspective is Fosco Maraini, *Meeting With Japan*, translated by Eric Mosbacher (New York: Viking, 1959). Tokyo University Professor Ishida Takeshi's *Japanese Society* (New York: Random House, 1971) is a gem of a book, highly recommended. The importance of hierarchical relations is effectively analyzed by Nakane Chie in her *Japanese Society* (Berkeley and Los Angeles: University of California Press, 1970).

Several general surveys of Japan's governmental system are (in alphabetical order): Ardath W. Burks, *The Government of Japan*, 2nd ed. (New York: Crowell, 1964); Nobutaka Ike, *Japanese Politics: Patron-Client Democracy* (New York: Knopf, 1972); Frank Langdon, *Politics in Japan* (Boston: Little, Brown, 1967); John M. Maki, *Government and Politics in Japan: The Road to Democracy* (New York: Praeger, 1962); Theodore McNelly, *Politics and Government in Japan*, 2nd ed. (Boston: Houghton Mifflin, 1972); Harold S. Quigley and John E. Turner, *The New Japan: Government and Politics* (Minneapolis: University of Minnesota Press, 1956); Warren M. Tsuneishi, *Japanese Political Style* (New York: Harper and Row, 1966); Robert E. Ward, *Japan's Political System* (Englewood Cliffs, N.J.: Prentice-Hall, 1967); and Chitoshi Yanaga, *Japanese People and Politics* (New York: Wiley, 1956). With one exception, each of these is available in paperback, and while each has a somewhat different emphasis, they all cover much of the same ground. The one hardcover book is Quigley and Turner's *The New Japan*, which provides the most complete coverage of both pre-Second World War and postwar Japanese governmental institutions. For an introduction to some recent Japanese intellectual history nothing is better than the analysis by an eminent Japanese political scientist, Maruyama

142

Bibliography

Masao, *Thought and Behavior in Modern Japanese Politics*, edited by Ivan Morris (New York: Oxford University Press, 1969).

Two books which provide basic descriptions of the Japanese Government prior to the Second World War are Charles B. Fahs, *Government in Japan* (New York: Institute of Pacific Relations, 1940), and Robert K. Reischauer, *Japan: Government — Politics* (New York: Nelson, 1939). A British journalist's illuminating view of the darker side of Japanese politics in the 1930s is Hugh Byas, *Government by Assassination* (London: Allen and Unwin, 1943).

Fujii Shin'ichi, *The Constitution of Japan, A Historical Survey* (Tokyo: Hokuseido, 1965) provides a distinctly Japanese interpretation of the Meiji (1890) and, much more briefly, the MacArthur (1947) Constitutions. An American scholar's analysis of the Meiji Constitution is George Akita, *Foundations of Constitutional Government in Modern Japan 1868—1890* (Cambridge, Mass.: Harvard University Press, 1967), which also contains an excellent chapter about the first Imperial Diet. Two long essays which are indispensable for an understanding of the Diet in the 1920s and early 1930s are Kenneth Colegrove's 'Parliamentary Government in Japan' (*American Political Science Review*, November 1927), and his 'Powers and Functions of the Japanese Diet' (*American Political Science Review*, December 1933 and February 1934). Less technical but fun to read are two books by Morgan Young, English foreign correspondent: *Japan under Taisho Tenno, 1912—1926* (London: Allen and Unwin, 1928), and *Imperial Japan* (London: Allen and Unwin, 1938).

Prewar party politics are brilliantly and exhaustively analyzed by Robert A. Scalapino in his *Democracy and the Party Movement in Prewar Japan: The Failure of the First Attempt* (Berkeley and Los Angeles: University of California Press, 1953). Also highly recommended are Tetsuo Najita, *Hara Kei in the Politics of Compromise, 1905—1915* (Cambridge, Mass.: Harvard University Press, 1967), and Peter Duus, *Party Rivalry and Political Change in Taishō Japan* (Cambridge, Mass.: Harvard University Press, 1968). Intellectual and ideological currents of the time are analyzed from various viewpoints in Joseph Pittau, S. J., *Political Thought in Early Meiji Japan* (Cambridge, Mass.: Harvard University Press, 1967); Nobutaka Ike, *The Beginnings of Political Democracy in Japan* (Baltimore: Johns Hopkins Press, 1950); and Arima Tatsuo, *The Failure of Freedom: A Portrait of Modern Japanese Intellectuals* (Cambridge, Mass.: Harvard University Press, 1969) — 'modern' in this instance meaning roughly the first quarter of this century.

E. Herbert Norman's *Japan's Emergence as a Modern State* (New York: Institute of Pacific Relations, 1940), and Sir George B. Sansom's *The Western World and Japan* (New York: Knopf, 1950) are both classics in their own right. They address themselves from very different perspectives to questions posed by Japan's 'modernization'. This topic was the subject of a series of conferences that were held in the 1960s the results of which are to be found in the Princeton University Press publications: Marius B. Jansen, ed., *Changing Japanese Attitudes Towards Modernization* (1965); William W. Lockwood, ed., *The State and Economic Enterprise in Japan* (1965); Ronald P. Dore, ed., *Aspects of Social Change in Modern Japan* (1967); Robert E. Ward, ed., *Political Development in Modern Japan* (1968); and James W. Morley, ed., *Dilemmas of Growth in Prewar Japan*

(1973). The foregoing is only the tip of an iceberg of materials dealing with Japan's modernization, a subject on which much has been written.

The Occupation era (1945–52) in Japanese politics, by comparison with 'modernization', is still relatively underdeveloped as a subject for serious scholarly research. This is partly the consequence of certain materials not yet being available because they remain classified. It is also partly the consequence of Japanese scholars having only begun (in the last five years) to do serious work on a Japanese experience which they perceive, understandably enough, as an issue hitherto too delicate for home consumption. An overview is provided by Kazuo Kawai in his *Japan's American Interlude* (University of Chicago Press, 1960), and in less organized form by Harry E. Wildes, an Occupation official, in his *Typhoon in Tokyo: The Occupation and Its Aftermath* (New York: Macmillan, 1954). Andrew Roth's, *Dilemma in Japan* (Boston: Little, Brown, 1945) is a fascinating projection of what was to be done with and to Japan after its defeat.

An early assessment of trends in Japanese politics under the Occupation is T. A. Bisson's *Prospects for Democracy in Japan* (New York: Macmillan, 1949). Robert A. Fearey in his *The Occupation of Japan, Second Phase: 1948–50* (New York: Macmillan, 1950) presents a sharply contrasting view. Robert B. Textor, *Failure in Japan* (New York: John Day, 1951) is stridently critical and laments missed opportunities for effectuating fundamental reforms. John D. Montgomery, *Forced to be Free: The Artificial Revolution in Germany and Japan* (University of Chicago Press, 1957) is the only study which attempts to compare, in broad outline, the intended re-shaping of Germany and Japan.

W. MacMahon Ball, the British Commonwealth representative on the Allied Council for Japan, provides an Australian judgment in his *Japan: Enemy or Ally?* (New York: John Day, 1949). Probably the best journalistic account of the initial Occupation years, in the sense of capturing the feel of the times, is Mark Gayn's *Japan Diary* (New York: William Sloane, 1948). Biographies of the American proconsul, for the greater part of the Occupation, General Douglas MacArthur have been written by two of his closest associates. Courtney Whitney, *MacArthur: His Rendezvous with History* (New York: Knopf, 1955), and Charles A. Willoughby, *MacArthur, 1941–51* (New York: McGraw-Hill, 1954) are highly partisan and adulatory, but contain some significant insights into the most important and most powerful Occupation official. Yoshida Shigeru, who served as Japan's Prime Minister for much of the Occupation era, has some pungent reflections on it all in his *The Yoshida Memoirs*, translated by his son Yoshida Ken'ichi (Boston: Houghton Mifflin, 1962).

The best generally available documentary collection of official Occupation policies and programs is in Volume II of *Political Reorientation of Japan, September 1945 to September 1948: Report of Government Section, Supreme Commander Allied Powers* (Washington, D.C.: Government Printing Office, 1949). Volume I of *Political Reorientation* contains a narrative history that is invaluable for gaining an understanding of how those who worked on many of the fundamental reform programs perceived Japan and what they believed they were accomplishing in its reorientation. Also valuable in this connection is Justin Williams, 'The Japanese Diet under the New Constitution', (*American Political Science Review*, October 1948).

Bibliography

A definitive study of the 1947 Constitution remains to be written. In the meantime, the following are useful as supplements to the official story as recounted in *Political Reorientation of Japan*: Dan F. Henderson, ed., *The Constitution of Japan — Its First Twenty Years, 1947–1967* (Seattle: University of Washington Press, 1968); John M. Maki, *Court and Constitution in Japan, Selected Supreme Court Decisions 1948–60* (Seattle: University of Washington Press, 1964); and Robert E. Ward, 'The Commission on the Constitution and Prospects for Constitutional Change in Japan' (*Journal of Asian Studies*, May 1965). A related, but broader, study is Arthur Taylor von Mehren, ed., *Law in Japan: The Legal Order in a Changing Society* (Cambridge, Mass.: Harvard University Press, (1964).

Specific Occupation reforms are analyzed in Ronald P. Dore, *Land Reform in Japan* (New York: Oxford University Press, 1959); T. A. Bisson, *Zaibatsu Dissolution in Japan* (Berkeley and Los Angeles: University of California Press, 1954); Eleanor M. Hadley, *Antitrust in Japan* (Princeton University Press, 1970); and Hans H. Baerwald, *The Purge of Japanese Leaders Under the Occupation* (Berkeley and Los Angeles: University of California Press, 1959).

The best general introduction to postwar Japan's political party system through the 1950s is Robert A. Scalapino and Masumi Junnosuke, *Parties and Politics in Contemporary Japan* (Berkeley and Los Angeles: University of California Press, 1962 — reissued in paperback, 1965). Three books are indispensable for a knowledge of the Liberal-Democratic Party — and much more; Nathaniel B. Thayer, *How the Conservatives Rule Japan* (Princeton University Press, 1969); Haruhiro Fukui, *Party in Power, The Japanese Liberal-Democrats and Policy-Making* (Berkeley and Los Angeles: University of California Press, 1970); and Gerald L. Curtis, *Election Campaigning Japanese Style* (New York: Columbia University Press, 1971). Equally indispensable for the major opposition party is Allan B. Cole, George O. Totten, and Cecil H. Uyehara, *Socialist Parties in Postwar Japan*, which should be read with its companion volume: George O. Totten, *The Social-Democratic Movement in Prewar Japan* (New Haven: Yale University Press, 1966). More specialized, but highly recommended, is J. A. A. Stockwin, *The Japanese Socialist Party and Neutralism: A Study of a Political Party and Its Foreign Policy* (London: Cambridge University Press, 1969). Robert A. Scalapino's *The Japanese Communist Movement 1920–1966* (Berkeley and Los Angeles: University of California Press, 1967) is the most complete study on the subject. Briefer and more up-to-date is Paul Langer, *Communism in Japan* (Stanford University Press, 1971). For a short essay, see Hans H. Baerwald, 'The Japanese Communist Party: Yoyogi and Its Rivals' in Robert A. Scalapino, ed., *The Communist Revolution in Asia* (Englewood Cliffs, N.J.: Prentice-Hall, 1969). There is as yet no study specifically devoted to the Komeitō (Clean Government Party). It can be best studied through the literature on its parent organization such as James H. White's *The Sōkagakkai and Mass Society* (Stanford University Press, 1970). All of these books provide some insight into factionalism in Japan's contemporary party politics, but the topic is still open for deeper analysis.

There are a few case studies which illuminate aspects of the political process in contemporary Japan. Probably the best is George R. Packard, *Protest in Tokyo: The Security Treaty Crisis of 1960* (Princeton University Press, 1966).

Bibliography

Thoughtful and penetrating is Herbert Passin's 'The Sources of Protest in Japan' (*American Political Science Review*, June 1962). Donald C. Hellmann uses a narrower focus than Packard in exploring *Japanese Domestic Politics and Foreign Policy: The Peace Agreement with the Soviet Union* (Berkeley and Los Angeles: University of California Press, 1969). A brief study which restricts itself to the parliamentary process is Hans. H. Baerwald, 'Nikkan Kokkai: The Japan-Korea Treaty Diet' in Lucian W. Pye, ed., *Cases in Comparative Politics: Asia* (Boston: Little, Brown, 1970). Much broader in scope is Ehud Harari's *The Politics of Labor Legislation in Japan* (Berkeley and Los Angeles: University of California Press, 1973). The best study of a pressure group making itself felt is William E. Steslicke's *Doctors in Politics: The Political Life of the Japan Medical Association* (New York: Praeger, 1973). Chitoshi Yanaga in his *Big Business in Japanese Politics* (New Haven: Yale University Press, 1968) explores, somewhat diffusely, an important set of relationships. Penetrating glimpses into a wide range of issues that have faced the Japanese people in the 1950s and early 1960s are to be found in Lawrence Olson's *Dimensions of Japan* (New York: American University Field Staff, 1963).

Several periodicals provide relatively up-to-date coverage of Japanese political developments. *Asian Survey* (Berkeley: University of California Press) is a monthly, and *Pacific Affairs* (Vancouver: University of British Columbia) is a quarterly; both are very useful. The world of Japanese intellectuals can be most easily entered through the pages of the *Japan Interpreter*, successor of the *Journal of Social and Political Ideas in Japan* (both available through the Japan Society, New York). *Japan Quarterly* (Tokyo: Asahi Shimbun-sha [Newspaper]) continues to be extremely useful. Japanese Foreign Ministry coverage of selected topics is to be found in *Japan Report* (New York: Consulate-General of Japan). The most readily available English language newspaper is *The Japan Times*, which comes in daily or weekly airmail and seamail editions. Invaluable sources for broader coverage are the 'Daily Summary of the Japanese Press', and 'Summaries of Selected Japanese Magazines'; both are issued in mimeographed form by the American Embassy in Tokyo. Unfortunately, budgetary restrictions limit their distribution in the United States to a few libraries and specialists.

Finally, I hope that those of you who have read all these suggestions will have the opportunity of going to Japan. Reading about the country, its people and politics may be enjoyable, but the living world of Japan remains endlessly fascinating. May you have the opportunity of experiencing it all yourself.

Index

Index

atives, 42—3; China and USSR and, 45—6, 70; finance of, 49; electoral gains by (1972), 54, 65, 84, 117; factionalism in, 70—1; boycotts opening of 1973 Diet, 74; joint candidates of JSP and (1972), 128
compartmentalism in Japanese society, 132—3
compromise: not possible on some issues, 87; concept of, not valued by Japanese, 106; no room in politics for, 124, 126
Congress of USA, used as model for Diet, 14, 88, 99, 134, 137
Congressional Legislative Reorganization Act (1946), 14, 15, 88
consensus: high value placed on, 45, 46, 115; between LDP leaders and bureau-crats on legislation, 123
conservative group of parties, 31, 40; chasm between progressive parties and, 44—5; seats held by (1961—73), 47
constituencies, multi-member: LDP and, 40; promote factionalism, 54—7, 70, 71, 128
Constitution, Meiji (1890), 1, 2, 121; weaknesses seen by SCAP in, 10
Constitution of 1947, 8—10, 11; provision for amendments to, 17; attitudes towards revision of, 44—5, 119, 139; no-war clause in, 119
Cooperative Party (later People's Cooperative Party), 30; seats won by (H. of Representatives), 32; votes for, 36; percentage of seats won by, and votes for, 42

dangerous thoughts, 4, 11
delaying tactics, of Opposition in Diet, 87, 108—12, 126
demilitarization and disarmament of Japan: SCAP policy of, 6; SCAP turns away from, 8; now a subject of dispute, 119
democracy, parliamentary: as SCAP objective for Japan, 6—7; split within SCAP on, 7—8
Democratic Party (conservative), 30, 48; votes for, (H. of Councillors) 24, (H. of Representatives) 36—7; seats won by (H. of Representatives), 32—3; per-centage of seats won by and votes for, 42, 43

Democratic Liberal Party (conservative), 18; seats won by, (H. of Councillors), 20, (H. of Representatives), 32—3; votes for (H. of Councillors) 24, (H. of Representatives), 36; as successor of Minseitō, 30; merged in LDP (1955), 30—1
Democratic Socialist Party (DSP), 31, 65, 116—17; seats won by, (H. of Council-lors) 23, 28, (H. of Representatives), 34—5, 47; votes for, (H. of Councillors) 27, (H. of Representatives), 38—9, 56; trade union support for, 41; percentage of seats won by and votes for (H. of Representatives), 42—3; joint candidates of Komeitō and (1972), 128
Diet, *see* Imperial Diet, National Diet
Diet Law (1947), 14—18; on convocation of Diet, 74n; on approval of legislation by Diet, 75; on presiding officers, 86—7; on committees, 88—9; on membership of committees, 93; on length of session, 106
Diet Strategy Committees of political parties, 84, 85, 86, 113; and committee appointments, 93
'directors' of committees, 93, 94, 108, 135
Discipline Committees of Diet, 90
Domei Kaigi (Japan Confederation of Labor), 41
Dōshi (Friends Party), 21, 25

Economic Development, Committee for: supports LDP, 41
Economic Organizations, Federation of: supports LDP, 41, 124
Eda Saburō, JSP faction leader, 66, 118
education, of members of 1972 Cabinet, 60—3
Education, Standing Committee of H. of Councillors on, 113
election to Imperial Diet (1942), 5
elections to National Diet: maximum term between, 18; under the Occupation, 30; expenses of campaigns for, 50, 127, 138; news media and, 122, 130; political parties and, 126—9
electoral districts, 54; disparity in size of, 40, 128
electoral system: for H. of Councillors, 18—19; for H. of Representatives, 54;

148

Index

151